The Apostle Paul wrote in  should never come by way lies. Flip has carefully and thoughtfully unraveled the devil's schemes around half-truths and their damning effects. I strongly recommend you read this volume to sharpen your ability to recognize truth from error and build your capacity to refute those who spin these five half-truths.

Dan Dumas

CEO of Red Buffalo, special advisor to the President of Southern Seminary and Faculty member, author of *Live Smart: Preparing for the Future God Wants for You*

Charles Spurgeon famously said, 'Discernment is not knowing the difference between right and wrong. It is knowing the difference between right and almost right.' This is sorely what is lacking today. In his book, *Five Half-Truths*, Flip Michaels tackles head-on five key truths regarding Scripture, authentic Christianity, the nature of God, the person of Christ, and the gospel. Frankly, these are not things we can afford to get wrong. These essential truths must be rightly divided and contended for, and Flip does just that. A helpful book!

Nate Pickowicz

Pastor of Harvest Bible Church, Gilmanton Iron Works, New Hampshire, author of *Reviving New England* and *Why We're Protestant*

The sinful heart of man perpetually craves excuses to ignore the authority of truth in their life, and the culture around us has provided ample opportunities to disregard objective realities. In an age of fake news and disinformation, skepticism has never been stronger—the cynicism of our age coupled with the sensibilities of the post-modern world has calcified many hardened hearts to even the possibility of eternal truth. This is the context in which the church has been called to proclaim the grace and truth of Christ. To this end, *Five Half-Truths* by Flip Michaels has provided the church with a clear and cogent resource for engaging a skeptical world with biblical truth. Each chapter delves into some of the most common objections to the claims of the Bible and provides a winsome defense of the whole truth. This simple and clear presentation of the Christian faith would make a wonderful discipleship resource to encourage believers in their faith or engage unbelievers in the questions they have about Christianity. I pray that everyone buys two copies of this book, one to read for themselves and one for a person in their life who has questions about the truth.

Paul Shirley

Pastor of Grace Community Church, Wilmington, Delaware, and author of *Irony of the Cross*

Because the whole truth matters, I wholeheartedly commend to you this excellent evangelistic and apologetic resource expertly written by my fellow pastor and friend, Flip Michaels. In this book, you will find a skillful refutation of modern day fallacies and a careful proclamation of the gospel that transforms lives.

David Cunningham

Lead Pastor, GraceLife Church, Annville, PA and Founder of Sports4Him

It has been said that a half truth is a whole lie. Variations of that idiom have been attributed to different people over the years. Despite its uncertain origins, nowhere is this more acute than in the realm of theology, for in no realm are the stakes higher. In his book, *Five Half-Truths*, Flip Michaels thoughtfully and biblically engages five half-truths that are widely believed by untold millions of people, many of whom claim to be Christians. Flip ably demonstrates that in believing these half-truths one's eternal soul is in grave peril. Matters of eternal consequence are not the place for ambiguity. *Five Half-Truths* is a robust yet immensely readable and understandable defense of the non-negotiable *whole* truths taught by the Bible, our response to which will determine where we spend eternity. If you are a seasoned believer, this book will encourage and equip you to 'give an answer for the hope that is within you' (1 Pet. 3:15). If you know of someone who is interested in eternal matters but expresses doubts about Christianity, please, get this book in his hands. I enthusiastically commend it to you.

Justin Peters

Founder of Justin Peters Ministries, justinpeters.org,
Seminar/DVD *Clouds Without Water: A Biblical Critique of the Word-Faith Movement*, and author of *Do Not Hinder Them: A Biblical Examination of Childhood Conversion*

This important book reminds us that truth is not determined by subjective human reasoning, but by our God of truth who reveals Himself in His all-sufficient Word. This book is an important work that will prove helpful to those who have been seduced by those who have humanized God's truth.

Mike Hess

National Representative of the General Association of Regular Baptist Churches

Wrong theology leads to wrong living. In this timely work, *Five Half-Truths*, Flip Michaels has presented a clear and concise manual on the dangers of believing half-truths and how that inevitably leads to wrong living. In a world where God's truth is readily dismissed and considered insufficient and irrelevant for the age, this work is a reminder that God's truth endures. Use this book often to remind yourself of right biblical thinking so that your mind may be renewed and your heart transformed.

Dustin W. Benge

Editor of *Expositor Magazine* and Lecturer for The Andrew Fuller Center for Baptist Studies

Flip Michaels, a man with his finger on the pulse of culture, has catalogued the principle half-truths and deceptive jargon that inform the present-day dismissal of Christianity—both in the academy and on the street. Then, through incisive logic, the author demonstrates that every half-truth is a subtle lie. And, on top of that, Flip winsomely provides the antidote with a marvelously down-to-earth defense of the Bible and Christian truth. *Five Half-Truths* is a gift to the church and a needy world.

R. Kent Hughes

Senior Pastor Emeritus of College Church in Wheaton and the John Boyer Professor of Evangelism and Culture at Westminster Seminary in Philadelphia

Michaels takes a collection of frequent offenders—theological truths that are square, but which have been stripped of their pointy parts and turned into soft circles. He then unpacks them, and tries to give you the whole truth back. If your view of God is too soft, too round, too watered-down, then read this book. It will challenge you by giving you the whole truth, and in that way it will give you back the real truth.

Jesse Johnson

Lead Teaching Pastor at Immanuel Bible Church in Springfield, VA; Associate Dean of The Master's Seminary in Washington, DC; and blogger at thecripplegate.com.

FIVE

HALF

TRUTHS

ADDRESSING THE MOST COMMON
MISCONCEPTIONS OF CHRISTIANITY

FOREWORD BY PHIL JOHNSON

FLIP MICHAELS

CHRISTIAN
FOCUS

Scripture quotations, unless otherwise indicated, are taken from the *New American Standard Bible®*, Copyright © 1960, 1962, 1963, 1968, 1971, 1972, 1973, 1975, 1977, 1995 by The Lockman Foundation. Used by Permission (www. Lockman.org).

Scripture quotations marked NIV taken from the *HOLY BIBLE, NEW INTERNATIONAL VERSION*. Copyright © 1973, 1978, 1984 by International Bible Society. Used by permission of Hodder & Stoughton Publishers, a member of the Hodder Headline Group. All rights reserved. "NIV" is a registered trademark of International Bible Society. UK trademark number 1448790.

Scripture quotations marked ESV are from The Holy Bible, English Standard Version, copyright © 2001 by Crossway Bibles, a publishing ministry of Good News Publishers. Used by permission. All rights reserved. ESV Text Edition: 2011.

Scripture quotations from the King James Version are marked KJV.

Scripture quotations marked HCSB are from the Holman Christian Standard Bible®. HCSB®. Copyright © 1999, 2000, 2002, 2003 by Holman Bible Publishers. Used by permission. Holman Christian Standard Bible®, Holman CSB®, and HCSB® are federally registered trademarks of Holman Bible Publishers.

Copyright © Flip Michaels 2018

paperback ISBN 978-1-5271-0232-3
epub ISBN 978-1-5271-0284-2
mobi ISBN 978-1-5271-0285-9

First published in 2018
by
Christian Focus Publications Ltd,
Geanies House, Fearn, Ross-shire
IV20 1TW, Scotland
www.christianfocus.com

Cover design by Rubner Durais

Printed and bound by

Bell & Bain, Glasgow.

CONTENTS

Soli Deo Gloria
Glory to God alone

Acknowledgements

I would like to thank my wife and children for their loving encouragement along the way to complete this project. Their sacrifices are many in ministry; and their support has always been constant with God's calling upon my life. A special thanks to my spiritual family at GraceLife Church in Annville, Pennsylvania, as they are a blessing from above. Also, I am indebted to Willie Mackenzie, Rosanna Burton, my editor Larry Dixon, and the superb staff at Christian Focus for making this personal desire a published reality.

FOREWORD

BY PHIL JOHNSON

John MacArthur once said, 'Half-truth? That's a lie. I'd rather they call it a half-lie. It's a lie intended to cover up or mislead.' Spurgeon would have agreed. He wrote, 'The whole truth is wholesome. But a part of the truth may mislead, and cause us to make as great errors as if we had believed a falsehood. Half the truth is a lie.'[1]

A half-truth is a deliberate pastiche of truth and falsehood, designed to have the appearance of candor and credibility while undermining, obscuring, or contradicting the real truth. Half-truths can be even more deadly than blatant lies because they deny the truth with such sinister subtlety.

Jesus called Satan 'a liar and the father of lies' (John 8:44). A careful reading of Scripture reveals that the devil is also grandmaster of the half-truth. If you study the recorded lies of Satan in the Bible, you will discover many of

---

1. Charles Haddon Spurgeon, *The Salt Cellars: Being a Collection of Proverbs, Together with Homely Notes Thereon*, (London: Passmore & Alabaster, 1889), 240.

them are furtive half-truths—deception and misdirection cleverly covered with a devious veneer of false sincerity. Sometimes Satan even fortified his falsehoods with partial, twisted, or out-of-context quotations taken from Scripture. That's how he put Christ to the test. He quoted Psalm 91:11-12, for example, in an attempt to persuade Jesus to kill himself. The devil told Him, 'If you are the Son of God, throw yourself down, for it is written, "He will command his angels concerning you," and "On their hands they will bear you up, lest you strike your foot against a stone"' (Matt. 4:6). While that promise in the psalm is true enough, it speaks of God's sovereign protection when bad things are done to us. It is not a guarantee that we won't be harmed if we commit willful transgressions or wanton acts of reckless mischief. And since Scripture expressly forbids us to put God to the test, it would be a radically foolish sin for anyone to jump from the pinnacle of the Temple in order to see whether God would send angels to avert disaster. So Jesus answered Satan's twisted half-truth with a simple quotation from Deuteronomy 6:16. 'Again it is written, "You shall not put the Lord your God to the test"' (Matt. 4:7).

The devil told Eve, 'When you eat of [the forbidden fruit] your eyes will be opened … knowing good and evil.' True. But he added, 'And you will be like God.' False. In fact, that's a damnable and damning lie. That one half-truth led to the fall of humanity and opened the door to all the evil in the material universe.

The key danger of half-truths is that they tend to make lies and errors seem good, or sound appealing. We live in an era when multitudes—including countless professing Christians—are perfectly willing to accept half-truths, especially in the realm of Bible doctrine and gospel preaching. Anyone who has ever tried to correct a popular but deadly theological error knows this to be the case. People claim they can 'eat the meat and spit out the bones.' But when a half-truth corrupts the gospel, the doctrine of Christ's incarnation, or any other cardinal Christian truth, 'eating the meat' from those bones is not a biblically sound or spiritually safe approach to dealing with error. See Galatians 1:8-9 or 2 John 7-11. There's a very good reason no one tries to harvest the meat from six-day-old roadkill.

Flip Michaels has produced this incredibly helpful resource to help readers untangle truth from error in five of the devil's most popular theological half-truths. I love the clarity and energy with which he writes. I love the skill with which he answers the enemy's falsehoods. And I love his obvious devotion to biblical truth. In a simple yet profound way he gives us the truth, the whole truth, and nothing but the truth. That, of course, is the only acceptable way to present biblical truth. I trust this book will have a very long shelf life, and I pray that it will reach a very large audience.

Phil Johnson
Executive Director of Grace to You, and a Pastor at Grace
Community Church in Sun Valley, California

May 2018

Introduction

Tracking Down the Truth

We all know at least three liars. Just look in the mirror and each of them will be revealed: me, myself, and I (also known as the 'unholy trinity').

The psalmist tells us, 'All men are liars' (Ps. 116:11). Undeniably, this indictment of mankind is true. Lucifer's lie is what seduced and initiated the separation of man from God in the Garden of Eden (Gen. 3:4-5)[1]; and it has sadly served as our model of 'truth-telling' ever since. All of humanity repeats it routinely. There is no wiggle room here. It is a reality none can deny. Each of us is far from exemption. We have all told at least one lie, therefore we are all liars.

Worse yet, we have learned to disguise our lying. Today's dishonesty is delivered in an assortment of shapes and sizes. Look and see if you recognize any of them: there is the truth stretched (an ambiguous lie), a promise broken (a lazy lie),

---

1. 'The serpent said to the woman, "You surely will not die! For God knows that in the day you eat from it your eyes will be opened, and you will be like God, knowing good and evil."'

plagiarism (a misleading lie), a fib (a little white lie), and an outright **BOLD-FACED** lie ('liar, liar, pants on fire!').

However the most dangerous and deceptive of them all is the half-truth—a kind of lie that is consciously and calculatingly misleading. There is a manipulative motive behind this crime. Something has been left out by the teller in order to deceive the hearer. J.I. Packer once remarked that 'a half-truth masquerading as the whole truth becomes a complete untruth.'[2] Yes, a half-truth is far more than an exaggeration or elaboration; it is a two-faced lie.

This occurs often when dealing with the truth claims of Scripture. Lies are told to turn maxims into myths. A 'truth-claim' is generated and predicated upon nothing but an individual's relativistic worldview—the ill-founded idea that truth is different for each person. What was once a sincere truth-seeking conversation quickly turns into a conversation stopper. When a half-truth is employed the dialogue is brought to a screeching halt. 'It may be true for you, but not for me.'[3]

With this in mind, I believe there are five major half-truths commonly used to deflect any-and-all consideration for the validity of the Bible, Christianity, God, Christ, and faith. They have been administered to persuade people (including myself) to discount and disregard the truth of

---

2. J.I. Packer, *A Quest for Godliness: The Puritan Vision of the Christian Life* (Wheaton: Crossway, 1994), 126.

3. For a helpful resource on responding to relativism see Paul Copan's book *True For You, But Not For Me* (Bloomington: Bethany House Publishers, 2009).

the gospel, by 'accepting too much [error] with too little discernment.'[4]

Much like what we see in our political landscape (regardless of where you lean), these half-truths have created a truth-denying society. Modern pluralistic lies are routinely regarded as truth without a single solitary rebuttal. The role of reason is being replaced by tainted presuppositions. There is a growing populous where error abounds and logic is in short supply.

The great preacher of old, C.H. Spurgeon, defined this search for truth as 'knowing the difference between right and almost right.'[5] Reread that quote. Take notice of the disparity between the two, as it is profound. You might say, 'Well, at least you're close,' but close only counts in horseshoes and hand-grenades! No, we must get this right. It is the disparity between 'the Spirit of truth and the spirit of error' (1 John 4:6). And so it is my deepest desire to see God use these pages to deliver what is 'right' to you.

Perhaps that is one of the very reasons you are holding this little book in your hands. You are sincerely seeking the truth. Thank you for making such a commitment to do so.[6] Turn the page to begin your reading journey. Each chapter will reveal a *half-truth*, then unveil the *whole truth*, followed by an explanation of its *whole meaning*.

---

4. John MacArthur, *Fool's Gold? Discerning Truth in an Age of Error* (Wheaton: Crossway, 2005), 19.

5. Charles Haddon Spurgeon as quoted by Ligon Duncan in Tim Challies, *Discipline of Spiritual Discernment* (Wheaton: Crossway, 2007), 1.

6. 'Be diligent to present yourself approved to God as a workman who does not need to be ashamed, accurately handling the word of truth… and you will know the truth, and the truth will make you free' (2 Tim. 2:15; John 8:32).

I have been praying for this moment. It is time that we expose together these five falsehoods to uncover what has been intentionally hidden. These half-truths have been used to keep us from learning the whole truth for far too long.

1
HALF-TRUTH #1:
THE BIBLE WAS WRITTEN BY MEN

CONCERNING THE BIBLE

A group of middle-school students are sitting in a circle on a classroom floor. The teacher hands one of the children a folded piece of paper with a phrase written on it: 'A dog will dig a deep hole to hide a big bone.' The first student leans left and begins to whisper this phrase into the next student's ear. That student then whispers what she believes to be the phrase she has heard into the next person's ear, and so on, and so on. Ear-to-ear the sentence is slowly being altered from truth into fiction.

'A dog will dig a deep hole to hide a big bone.'
'A dog digs holes looking for his only bone.'
'A dog is lost from a loving home.'
'A dog has learned to use the telephone.'

By the time the statement has reached its final destination, it has been completely misinterpreted and manufactured into something that sounds nothing like the original. Do you remember playing the telephone game? It is a great ice-breaker for parties. However, there are some who believe it has been played out in the spiritual realm, too—a game where common circumstances have been transformed into miraculous moments—you know, like those we read of in the Bible. Something simple occurs, but when you add a listening ear, and stir the story gently over time—voilà! The truth has become fiction. What was sound is now superficial.

Let me illustrate such a scenario; here is an example from the Bible. One late evening approximately two thousand years ago, Jesus had decided to withdraw from the crowds, which had included His own disciples. He desired to be in prayer—to be left alone to commune with His Father before entering the next important stage of His ministry. And so He sends the twelve into a boat to make their way to Capernaum, which is on the other side of the Sea of Galilee. One of His disciples, Matthew, explains further in his own Gospel:

> Immediately He made the disciples get into the boat and go ahead of Him to the other side, while He sent the crowds away. After He had sent the crowds away, He went up on the mountain by Himself to pray; and when it was evening, He was there alone. But the boat was already a long distance from the land, battered by the waves; for the wind was contrary. And in the fourth watch of the night He came to them, walking on the sea. When the disciples saw Him walking on the sea, they were terrified, and said,

'It is a ghost!' And they cried out in fear. But immediately Jesus spoke to them, saying, 'Take courage, it is I; do not be afraid.' Peter said to Him, 'Lord, if it is You, command me to come to You on the water.' And He said, 'Come!' And Peter got out of the boat, and walked on the water and came toward Jesus. But seeing the wind, he became frightened, and beginning to sink, he cried out, 'Lord, save me!' Immediately Jesus stretched out His hand and took hold of him, and said to him, 'You of little faith, why did you doubt?' When they got into the boat, the wind stopped. And those who were in the boat worshiped Him, saying, 'You are certainly God's Son!' (Matt. 14:22-33).

Does the telephone game effectively explain away a miracle such as this? Did Jesus really walk on top of the stormy waves to meet His weary disciples some three miles off the shore? Or could this message have somehow lost its original meaning over the years? Maybe by multiple tellings over a significant period of time (person-to-person-to-person-to-person) Jesus' actions were altered from walking *by* the sea and skipping stones to walking *on* it and stopping the wind?

If that were true, then a person could argue that the biblical account is a false one. Sure, the wind was blowing and the dawn would soon rise. But Jesus was simply enjoying His meditative time by the sea, skipping stones, knowing that a new day would begin with the shining of the sun.

Stop right there. Most people would not dispute that data. It is a reasonable series of events. They would agree that it is highly probable a man named Jesus lived two thousand years ago (we'll address this specifically in chapter four); that the Sea of Galilee, today called the 'Kinneret,' is well-known for its windy waters; and that Jesus likely would have had a solitary stroll along the shore skipping stones before dawn. It would have been breathtakingly beautiful, with an advancing aurora behind some cumulonimbus clouds—likely worthy of a social media post!

Yet that is not what the Bible tells us. Instead, it says that 'He came to them, walking *on* the sea' (Matt. 14:26, emphasis mine). Remember here, the Bible's claim is that Jesus *literally* walked on wave after wave to get to the disciples' boat.

Which version will you believe?

Pick any miracle of the Bible and you will be faced with the exact same question:

- The Creation Account—did man alter the universe's 'Big Bang' to 'in the beginning'?

- The Global Flood—was it a limited and local event inflated to cover the entire planet?

- The Parting of the Red Sea— what if it was only a good wind and the Israelites had good timing?

- The Feeding of 5,000— doesn't it seem like this supper was excessively exaggerated?

- The Death and Resurrection of Christ—maybe He was unconscious, having never died?

Clearly, each of these examples point to the same problem. They are either on the side of truth or fiction. Are they a collection of unembellished and unvarnished realities? Or merely an assortment of doubtful and dubious dogmas? This is why it is vital for us to understand how the Bible became *the* Bible. We need to know what, if any, evidence points to an accurate transmission of the biblical accounts over time. Is it reliable and viable? Can we trust what is in our possession today as the authoritative and unadulterated truth?

THE HALF-TRUTH

THE BIBLE WAS WRITTEN BY MEN.

In much the same way we play the telephone game, a claim is being made that there is an assortment of fairy tales bound together over thousands of years. Sacred texts seen as nothing more than historical exaggerations. Yes, some do regard them collectively as the 'Holy Bible,' but there are others who do not believe this book to be holy, nor *the* Bible. There is nothing spectacular or supernatural to be found here. A man-made book that is unique in its creativity, and valuable in some of its maxims, but that is all.

First, what this half-truth implies is that the Bible is unholy and unsound. No book written by a bunch of old men is supernatural, nor is it error-free. These accounts are likely the victim of the telephone game played out over centuries. Call them legends, but in no way can they be regarded as the literal words of God, supernaturally communicated to mankind, as a guidebook for life and all eternity. A person would have to be crazy to unequivocally believe this. 'Better check your meds, because you are leaving me plenty of room for doubt.'

Second, what is also being implied here is the idea there is no such thing as absolute truth—let alone an exclusive one. This worldview declares that *no book* can make such a declaration. There is no reason to treat the Bible as an authentic or historical account, nor should we give it our undivided attention, because all truth is relative. Only the naïve would hold to such a narrow view that the Bible is the lone source of revelation from God to all humanity. 'Come on, man, I wasn't born yesterday!'

A third and final implication as a result of the telephone game is that there are numerous contradictions and outright errors in the Bible, and many intellectuals have committed significant time and energy to prove what we already know: this is a book of myths contradicting both science and history. Moreover, a number of its moral judgments are outdated and rarely, if ever, are they applicable to our various contemporary cultures. The academia of today concur: a fully-grown adult would have to be delusional to rely upon this distorted document as their standard of truth. 'Just open your eyes. Do you not see that our reality contradicts your rationale?'

THE WHOLE-TRUTH

*THE BIBLE WAS WRITTEN BY MEN **AND INSPIRED BY** GOD.*

First, it must be acknowledged that what we would call Scripture (e.g., the Bible, God's Word) contains sixty-six books, 1,189 chapters, 31,173 verses, and 774,746 words.[1] Its human origin cannot be denied, as it was penned by over forty different authors. These men came from all walks of life—kings, prophets, a fisherman, a tax-collector, a former

---

1. John MacArthur, *The NASB MacArthur Study Bible* (Nashville: Thomas Nelson, 2006), 'How We Got the Bible' xvii.

Pharisee—representing three different continents, writing in three different languages, over a period of 1,600 years.

Yet that is only half the truth. Not only did men pen those words, but it was God who gave those words to them to write with perfect precision. That is the second half of the truth. 'All Scripture is inspired by God' (2 Tim. 3:16). God is the divine Author, having revealed His will to each of these men. The message they would be inspired to write would originate from the indomitable mind of the Almighty.

The Greek word for 'inspired' in this verse is *theopneustos*. It originates from two words, *theós* meaning 'God,' and *pnéō* 'to breathe out.' Literally, God exhaled! He breathed out one seamless Book with one singular message over nearly two thousand years of human history. It is one-of-a-kind. This Book of books holds within its pages many cultures, languages, and historical events; and each of these human dimensions was the vehicle in which God gave His breathed-out words to man. The only perfect or pure book you will ever hold in your hand is the B-I-B-L-E, the very Word of God.

THE WHOLE MEANING

If the whole truth is that God revealed His words to man and divinely guided the process of writing and preserving the Bible, then the telephone game is an ignorant effort to dismiss this supernatural Book of wisdom. Could they have been embellished stories? Nope. Were they somehow exaggerated accounts? I am afraid not. We cannot make these kinds of claims, at least not truthfully. We are in no position to reject the Bible, for the whole truth tells us otherwise. There is a greater meaning than that of today's popular mythology. There is a purpose found within its pages.

Prolific author and seminary professor D. A. Carson states it best when he writes, 'rather, such Scripture was the product of human authors and the revelation of the God who talks. What Scripture said, God said… for its words are God's words.'[2] The implications here are considerable. They should hit us like a caffeine crash. If this is not merely man's words—but God's—then how do we handle it? Carefully. Are we to esteem it? Highly. Can we trust it? Completely. Should we obey it? Submissively.

Certainly, how we regard the Bible matters, but I am getting ahead of myself.

At this point I assume you will want to see any-and-all historical data that would support such a claim of the Bible having been written by men *and* inspired by God. The whole truth demands an explanation. And I understand your concern. Many 'truth-tellers' are far from being just that, a teller of truth. But where do we begin?

We must first ask for some accounting of the relationship between God's verbal revelation and its product produced by human hands.[3] It is one thing to declare the whole truth, but altogether another to do the heavy-lifting and unpack its meaning. Rhetoric without reason is a poor attempt at persuasion. Simply stated, it is manipulation.[4]

---

2. D.A. Carson, *Collected Writings on Scripture* (Wheaton: Crossway, 2010), 28.

3. Ibid, 31.

4. In J.P. Moreland's book, *Love Your God with All Your Mind: The Role of Reason in the Life of the Soul* (Colorado Springs: NavPress, 1997), he challenges this practice of rhetorical manipulation when he says, 'Because of the mindlessness of our culture, people do not persuade others of their views (religious or otherwise) on the basis of argument of reason, but rather, by

Fair enough. Let's pull this car over to the side of the road to examine what is being said rationally. We will do this by looking at four primary elements: the *activity* involved in how we have received Scripture, then the *authenticity* of the documents of the Bible, followed by the *accuracy* of the details contained within its pages, and ending with the impact of its *authority* as the very Word of God.

ACTIVITY

Let's face it: the activity—the process that communicated and caused the Bible—will have to be significant and supernatural if it is to live up to the unique claim of being the literal Word of God. And it truly is, having all originated from one Source, God. When exploring this process, it will be helpful for us to become acquainted with a few new theological terms (revelation, verbal, plenary, and inspiration).

As stated earlier in this chapter, it was God who revealed His will to man. The *revelation* of God is a special revelation (as opposed to a natural one—i.e., nature), in that it is a divine self-disclosure of His will. Peter describes this activity in 2 Peter 1:20-21, 'no prophecy of Scripture is a matter of one's own interpretation, for no prophecy was ever made by an act of human will, but men moved by the Holy Spirit spoke from God.' So yes, it is true that men wrote each book (e.g., Peter penned 1 Peter), but it was God through

---

expressing emotional rhetoric and politically correct buzzwords. Reason has given way to rhetoric, evidence to emotion, substance to slogan, the speech writer to the makeup man, and rational authority (the right to command compliance and to be believed) to social power (the ability to coerce compliance and outward conformance).'128.

His Spirit that determined and directed the Word of God, thereby protecting it from error.

Think about it. Every single word that was given to man over those 1,600 years fits perfectly into a miraculous puzzle. What is in our possession came directly from God. Not one word is out of place, 'not the smallest letter or stroke' (Matt. 5:18). There is no other book that can make this assertion; and the Bible's authors repeatedly attest to this phenomenon.

Pointing to Moses in the Old Testament, God declares, 'I will raise up a prophet from among their countrymen like you, and *I will put My words in his mouth*, and he shall speak to them all that I command him' (Deut. 18:18, emphasis mine). In the New Testament, dealing with the birth of Christ, we read, 'Now all this took place to fulfill what was *spoken by the Lord through the prophet* [Isaiah]: "Behold, the virgin shall be with child and shall bear a Son, and they shall call His name Immanuel," which translated means, "God with us"' (Matt. 1:22-23, emphasis mine).

Stay with me here. This is also what we call *verbal, plenary inspiration*. Verbal, in that God gave these men every single word; plenary, emphasizing that all of the words—His words—have equal authority (not just a concept or the 'red letter' words of Jesus); and inspiration, meaning that God divinely guided the process and its preservation. Again, verbal, plenary inspiration.

So who wrote the book of Romans—God or the apostle Paul? Paul wrote it, but God inspired it. (A trick question!) You see, the writers weren't inspired; their message was. The apostle wrote it with his quill in his own surroundings, but it was the Spirit of God that gave him those words. In fact, the writers of the Bible testify to having recorded God's actual words a staggering 3,808 times.[5] David, for example, wrote in 2 Samuel 23:2, 'The Spirit of the LORD spoke by me, and His word was on my tongue.' The words that were written were the exact ones God wanted. They did not originate in a human author's mind. They were breathed out (remember, *theopneustos* 'inspired') by God. He sovereignly superintended the entire process, including the providential oversight of every human author's life. He prepared them. Their words are really His words.[6]

In his classic work, *The Inspiration and Authority of the Bible*, B.B. Warfield argued, 'When Paul declares, then, that "every scripture," or "all scripture" is the product of divine breath, [that it] "is God-breathed," he asserts with as much energy as he could employ that Scripture is the product of a specifically Divine operation.'[7] Amen, and that divine activity is known as inspiration. This is how we have come to receive the life-giving message found within its pages.

AUTHENTICITY

Not only is the (divine) activity impressive, but the authenticity of these documents are equally so. Actually, many of

---

5. John MacArthur, *Focus on the Fact* (New York City: Revell Company, 1977), 45.

6. I appreciate how Steven Cowan and Terry Wilder explain this, 'This does not mean that God mechanically dictated the words of the Bible to its human authors… God inspired the Bible by providentially preparing the human writers through their upbringing, education, and life experiences so that when they wrote, their words were their words. And yet, they were also God's words because they wrote what God intended for them to write.' *In Defense of the Bible: A Comprehensive Apologetic for the Authority of Scripture* (Nashville, B&H Publishing Group, 2013), 4-5.

7. B.B. Warfield, *The Inspiration and Authority of the Bible* (Louisville, SBTS Press, 2014), 133.

them are now in our possession. God has exceedingly protected and preserved His Word throughout the millennia. While many ancient books might boast about the discovery of five or even ten copies, the Bible has thousands at its fingertips.

The original documents (or manuscript evidence) that make up the Bible are arranged by books—there are sixty-six in all with thirty-nine in the Old Testament and twenty-seven in the New. Specific to the New Testament, there are approximately 5,700 copies in existence today and they significantly surpass any other ancient manuscript in count.

The manuscripts are made up of either papyrus or parchment. Some contain merely a word or phrase, others a portion of a letter or even an entire testament. While none of the originals (called 'autographs') are in existence, the volume of manuscript copies in hand has allowed textual scholars to reconstruct the originals. A few of the fragments date back to within 25-50 years of the autographs, resulting in 99.99% of them having been reclaimed.[8]

These numbers are astounding! To deny the authenticity of the Bible is to deny many of the books we were required to read in college. No kidding. Were you ever assigned Sophocles' *Tragedies*, Caesar's *Gallic Wars*, or any one of Plato's seven *Tetralogies*? None of these classics from antiquity are able to make that same 99.99% claim. Only Homer's *Iliad* comes close, with over 1,800 manuscripts and a 95% score.[9] If you believe in the legitimacy and reliability

---

8. MacArthur, *The NASB MacArthur Study Bible*, 'How We Got the Bible' xxi. By the way, there is no cardinal doctrine at stake in the missing .01%.

9. Thanks in large part to new archeological discoveries, many of these numbers continue to be updated and can be accessed online: http://www.

of the writings of Sophocles, Caesar, and Plato, then you've also got to acknowledge the authenticity of the Bible. To reject one is to reject all others. What choice does the intellectual have but to affirm the authenticity of the Bible? It has been said that 'in contrast with these figures [from the works of antiquity], the textual critic of the New Testament is embarrassed by a wealth of material.'[10]

And again, we have only dealt with the New Testament. However, the Old Testament is directly quoted by the New at least 320 times.[11] The original audiences of the New Testament recognized the canon (the collection of authoritative writings) of the Old, and did so without a doubt. New Testament writer after writer points to an author of the Old. In Romans 9:29, the apostle Paul wrote, 'And just as Isaiah foretold;' and again in 10:19, 'Moses says…' Jesus Himself was no exception when referencing the Old Testament, having quoted from the book of Psalms eleven times, Deuteronomy ten times, Isaiah eight times, and Exodus seven times.

Four paragraphs. That is all I have written here in support of the authenticity of the Scriptures; and (as I'm sure you now

---

josh.org/wp-content/uploads/Bibliographical-Test-Update-08.13.14.pdf.

10. Bruce M. Metzger and Bart D. Ehrman, *The Text of the New Testament: Its Transmission, Corruption, and Restoration 4th ed.* (New York: Oxford, 2005), 51. They continue, 'Furthermore, the work of many ancient authors has been preserved only in manuscripts that date from the Middle Ages (sometimes the late Middle Ages), far removed from the time at which they lived and wrote. On the contrary, the time between the composition of the books of the New Testament and the earliest extant copies is relatively brief. Instead of a lapse of a millennium or more, as is the case of not a few classical authors, several papyrus manuscripts of portions of the New Testament are extant that were copied within a century or so after the composition of the original documents.'

11. Henry M. Morris, *Many Infallible Proofs, 19th ed.* (Green Forest: Master Books, 2010), 57.

see) the evidence is overwhelmingly sufficient. Arguing in favor of the trustworthiness of the New Testament, Daniel B. Wallace describes the bewildering attitudes of those who continue, in light of the evidence, to refuse to acknowledge its authenticity:

> Precisely because we have hundreds of thousands of variants *and* hundreds of *early manuscripts*, we are in an excellent position for recovering the wording of the original. Further, if the radical skeptics applied their principles to the rest of Greco-Roman literature, they would thrust us right back into the Dark Ages, where ignorance was anything but bliss. Their arguments only sound impressive in a vacuum.[12]

We have looked at the (divine) activity in receiving God's Word—namely that God revealed His written will to man through the process of inspiration; and we have also surveyed the (superior) claims of its authenticity. This included the manuscript evidence of the New, and the corroboration of the Old with the direct testimonies of Jesus Christ and the apostle Paul. What's the next step? We must address the Bible's accuracy.

ACCURACY

Anecdotally speaking, one of the most common attacks against the validity of the Bible is also one of the weakest. To say that 'the Word of God is not really the Word of God because it is inaccurate' is easy to dismantle. Why? Because this gets at the crux of the Bible, its content. All you would

---

12. Cowan and Wilder, *In Defense of the Bible: A Comprehensive Apologetic for the Authority of Scripture*, 151-52.

need to do is to read through your Bible to help the individual see that he or she is wrong in their assessment. And this is usually my first question in response to the person, 'Have you ever read the Bible for yourself?'

The late great theologian, Dr. R.C. Sproul, tells a similar story of a conversation he had after being asked, 'How can you believe that the Bible is inerrant when [it] is filled with contradictions?'[13]

> I said, 'What did you say?' He said, 'It is filled with contradictions.' 'Let me give you a challenge,' I said. 'That's a pretty big book, sixty-six books. If it's filled with contradictions it shouldn't be difficult to find a few. Let me give you this challenge, it's one o'clock this afternoon, I am going to meet you here tomorrow at one o'clock, and I want you to give me a list of fifty contradictions in the Bible. You ought to be able to find them with ease between now and twenty-four hours if this book is filled with them.'
>
> 'Okay, I'll take that up.' So on the next day the guy comes back at one o'clock... and he's telling me he was up all night, he's bleary eyed... [but] he had a list of thirty. I said, 'I asked you for fifty? Not as many in there as you thought, right? But thirty, that's enough to get rid of inerrancy, no question about that. So let's look at them one at a time.' And we looked at each passage of those thirty, one after another, where I was able to show him... to his satisfaction, that not one of them violated the law of noncontradiction [where contradictory statements cannot both be true in the same sense at the same time].

---

13. Taken from *Q&A with R.C. Sproul & Ligonier Teaching Fellows (May 19, 2011)*, Ligonier Ministries, https://youtube/xnTSjntQzjY. I would encourage you to listen to this story in its entirety, 50:00-54:00.

Sproul's point is an important one: Scripture will never contradict Scripture. Reading this Book (or any book for that matter) in its true context will always help to bring clarity. Often verses are cherry-picked with no regard for the author's audience in an attempt to misappropriate them and abuse God's Word. Again, this tactic is an easy one to refute. Read your Bible.

But what if we were to take this line of thinking one step further? What if it could be shown that the historical persons, events, and locations are also accurate? That the archeological discoveries of the past and present continue to ratify its reliability? And that the science mentioned within its pages is not only provable, but often proclaimed prior to man's own discoveries? Then the half-truth of the telephone game would hold absolutely no water, right?

Not a drop. Why? Because we never-ever find something shared in the telephone game returning full circle intact, unaltered, and totally accurate.

Challenge accepted! We can begin by examining the Bible historically. Not as historical fiction—where real events and even persons are used to create an entirely new storyline. Instead, we want to look briefly at two fascinating finds (using archeology) to support the Bible's claims of accuracy. Below are what I believe to be two of the very best—sitting atop a plethora of archaeological dig discoveries.

The first find is called a 'bulla.' A lump of clay used to seal a manuscript or a deed. You have likely seen a bulla in a movie—representing a royal seal. The outside of the message would have an impression (or even a fingerprint) from say, the king, to officially seal and protect his document from prying eyes. Bullae were used in biblical times, too. So to come across such a seal would represent a sensational find.

What if you were to learn that not one, ten, or even fifty of these had been discovered, but four hundred?! That kind of evidence would be overwhelming. Old Testament scholar Walter Kaiser, Jr. places a high premium on these finds: 'Some 400 seal inscriptions have been found, most of them dating from the eighth to the sixth century B.C. These seals are the equivalents of finding the personal signatures of these Old Testament persons.'[14]

Specifically, one of the most exciting bullae to be unearthed was the discovery of Baruch's seal in 1975. Baruch had transcribed all of Jeremiah's words according to Jeremiah 36:4, 'Then Jeremiah called Baruch the son of Neriah, and Baruch wrote on a scroll at the dictation of Jeremiah all the words of the LORD which He had spoken to him.'

The second ancient artifact that attracts our attention is called the 'stele.' These were upright slabs or stones used as monuments. They would have an inscribed surface used to mark an important event, such as a military victory. One such archeological find was noted within the pages of the esteemed *Biblical Archeology Review*, 'Few modern biblical archaeology discoveries have caused as much excitement as the Tel Dan inscription—writing on a ninth-century

---

14. Cowan and Wilder, *In Defense of the Bible: A Comprehensive Apologetic for the Authority of Scripture,* 214-15. Moreover, 'Archaeology has been one of the strongest allies for making the case for the historical accuracy of the Old Testament... they have repeatedly provided an almost uncanny confirmation of the accuracy of the history of the Old Testament.' 220.

B.C. stone slab (or stela) that furnished the first historical evidence of King David from the Bible.'[15]

Found in 1993, this fragment has an expression, 'House of David,' carved on it which affirms that the dynasty of King David really did exist. The Biblical Archaeology Society wrote in the same publication that 'The stela's fragmented inscription … proved that King David from the Bible was a genuine historical figure and not simply the fantastic literary creation of later biblical writers and editors. Perhaps more importantly, the stela, set up by one of ancient Israel's fiercest enemies more than a century after David's death, still recognized David as the founder of the kingdom of Judah.'[16]

Deep dive into the field of biblical archaeology and you will discover exciting finds like these supporting the Bible's accuracy. From a historical perspective, we are left with no other choice than to take God at His word. History in the Bible has nothing to do with historical-fiction. And the same can be said about science in the Bible, as it has nothing to do with science-fiction.

Herbert Spencer was a nineteenth century scientist who died in 1903. His scientific career was recognized for one singular achievement, a summation that all reality, everything that exists in the universe, can be placed into five categories: time, force, action, space and matter. His assertion was that nothing could exist outside of these categories. But there seems to be a slight problem with his discovery—Genesis 1:1 beat him to it! 'In the beginning'

---

15. '"David" Found at Dan,' *Biblical Archeology Review: 20:2.* March/April 1994. 26.

16. Ibid.

(time), 'God' (force), 'created' (action), 'the heavens' (space) 'and the earth' (matter). All Mr. Spencer had to do was open his Bible. All anyone had to do was read the first verse of the first chapter of the first book.[17]

Another scientific breakthrough dealt with the continuous movement of water (above, on, and below the surface of the earth), otherwise known as the hydrological cycle. An original mass of water has, for centuries, gone through the cycle of evaporation, transpiration, precipitation and irrigation, only to run off and begin the entire process all over again. Man did not begin to understand this concept of hydrology until the seventeenth century. Guess what? This principle is also found throughout the Bible. Job 36:27-28 reads, 'For He draws up the drops of water, they distill rain from the mist, which the clouds pour down, they drip upon man abundantly'; and another, Isaiah 55:10 adds, 'For as the rain and the snow come down from heaven, and do not return there without watering the earth.'

These stories are persuasive, are they not? Here are two additional accounts.

In 1628, William Harvey had learned by studying anatomy and physiology that the circulation of blood is vital to life. This was big, as he was the first physician to do so. Yet again, the Bible stated this much, much earlier. Leviticus 17:11 reads, 'For the life of the flesh is in the blood.'

In 1639, it was rightfully predicted that Venus had a fixed orbit, which would result in the planet traveling in front of the sun every two years. Indeed, their conjecture was

---

17. John MacArthur, *The Battle for the Beginning: Creation, Evolution and the Bible* (Nashville: Thomas Nelson, 2001), 40-41.

correct, but the principle had already been shared long, long ago in Jeremiah 31:35, 'Thus says the LORD, Who gives the sun for light by day and the *fixed order* of the moon and the stars for light by night' (emphasis mine).

Whichever path you choose, by examining the accuracy of God's Word as it relates to history or to science, you will find on your journey that both roads lead to the same conclusion: the Bible's content can be trusted. It is entirely accurate and can be trusted wholeheartedly. However, this then presents us with one remaining problem to solve—authority. Does the Bible really have the right to impose its values upon our way of life?

AUTHORITY

Let us quickly review: activity, authenticity, and accuracy. If we agree that God spoke His divine will to and through men to be written down—an *activity* of special revelation through inspiration—and we accept the overwhelming body of material in our possession as indisputably *authentic*, as well as historically and scientifically *accurate*, then we are only left with a rhetorical question: does it deserve the title 'The Word of God'?

This question is a rhetorical one because it rests upon the character of God. To say that God wrote those words is to say that it bears the weight of His authority. Its words are His words and they are trustworthy because He is trustworthy. When the Bible states that 'God... cannot lie' (Titus 1:2), it is also pronouncing that what is written in the Bible is 'the faithful word... sound doctrine' (1:9).

J.I. Packer makes this same point in his book *Fundamentalism and the Word of God*. He writes,

> The scriptural approach to Scripture is thus to regard it
> as God's written testimony to Himself. When we call the
> Bible the Word of God, we mean, or should mean, that its
> message constitutes a single utterance of which God is
> the author. What Scripture says, He says. When we hear or
> read Scripture… [it] is the speech of God Himself.[18]

Many have continued to argue that while it may be okay
to personally declare Scripture as 'the Word of God,' this in
no way implies a person can impose it upon a segment of
society. Especially when that segment chooses to disregard
it as having originated from the One True God.

The position is better known as moral relativism—
where the truth can be contradictory, contextual, and
culture-bound. In other words, it does not matter to that
person what you believe. They would say, 'Just because you
believe does not mean I must do the same. A universal truth
cannot be known nor does it even exist. Your religion can
be true for you and untrue for me.' But here is the real rub
to that kind of thinking. A philosophical fallacy is standing
in the way. You see, a relativist will not remain a relativist
when his rights are being violated.

A story is told of an argument over moral relativism that
took place in a dorm room at the University of Vermont.[19]

> The student began to espouse… 'What is true for you is
> true for you and whatever is true for me is true for me.
> If something works for you because you believe it, that's

---

18. J.I. Packer, *Fundamentalism and the Word of God* (Grand Rapids: Inter-Varsity Press, 1958), 89.

19. J.P. Moreland, *Love Your God with All Your Mind: The Role of Reason in the Life of the Soul* (Colorado Springs: NavPress, 1997), 153.

great. But no one should force his or her views on other people since everything is relative.' […]

I picked up his small stereo and started out the door with it. 'Hey, what are you doing?' he shouted.

'What's wrong with you?' I queried. 'Are you having problems with your eyes? I am leaving your room with your stereo.'

'You can't do that,' he gushed.

'Well,' I replied, 'since I lift weights and jog regularly, I think I can in fact do it without any help. But maybe you meant to say, 'You *ought not* do that because you are stealing my stereo.' Of course, I know from our previous conversation that this is not what you mean. I happen to think it is permissible to steal stereos if it will help a person's religious devotions, and I myself could use a stereo to listen to Christian music in my morning devotions. Now I would never try to force you to accept my moral beliefs in this regard because, as you said, everything is relative and we shouldn't force our ideas on others. But surely you aren't going to force on me your belief that it is wrong to steal your stereo, are you? You know what I think? I think that you espouse relativism in areas of your life where it's convenient, say in sexual morality, or in areas about which you do not care, but when it comes to someone stealing your stereo or criticizing your own moral hobbyhorses, I suspect you become a moral absolutist pretty quickly, don't you?'

Indeed, each of us have a moral compass. We really are 'moral absolutists.' It is unavoidable, inescapable, and to deny such a thing is to acknowledge it. This truth touches us all. Everything we think, say, or do is either right or wrong; and there are absolute standards to determine its morality.

You have been armed with a lot in this chapter.

You now know that the Bible is not the result of a telephone game that has been haphazardly played out over two millennia. So which truth will you choose to believe? The half-truth: the Bible was written by men, or the whole truth: the Bible was written by men *and inspired by God*. The 'prince of preachers' Charles Haddon Spurgeon once bellowed his choice from a London pulpit, 'I would rather speak five words out of this Book than 50,000 words of the philosophers!'[20]

SUMMARY

- **The Half-Truth:** the Bible was written by men. Sure, it sounds good, but that is the only thing sound about it. In much the same way we play the telephone game, this statement presupposes that the Bible is an assortment of fairy tales bound together over millennia.

- **The Whole-Truth:** the Bible was written by men *and inspired by God*. Not only did men pen those words, but it was God who gave His Word to them to write with perfect precision; He revealed His will to each man. The divine Author literally 'breathed-out' one seamless Book with one singular message to over forty authors spanning nearly two thousand years of human history.

- **The Whole Meaning:** God spoke His divine will to and through men to be written down—an *activity* of special revelation through (verbal, plenary) inspiration; and we accept the overwhelming body of material in

---

20. Preached by Charles Haddon Spurgeon on March 6, 1892; no. 2246. 'Come From the Four Winds, O Breath!' *The Metropolitan Tabernacle Pulpit, Vol. 38* (Edinburgh: The Banner of Truth Trust, 1991).

our possession as indisputably *authentic* (i.e., 99.99% of the manuscripts); they are historically and scientifically *accurate* (via man's archaeological and observational discoveries); and because its words are His words, it deserves to be called 'The Word of God,' bearing the full weight of His *authority*.

2
HALF-TRUTH #2:
ALL RELIGIONS ARE THE SAME

CONCERNING CHRISTIANITY

If you have ever watched a courtroom drama, then you know how enormously important the evidence can be. Accurate information leads, guides, directs, and even teaches the jury so that they may form a conviction. Discerning listeners make for good jurors. By using their analytical skills they are usually able to put together the evidential puzzle and render a right decision.

But consider for a moment the consequences of getting a verdict wrong. We have all heard of a wrongly convicted felon—the poor soul who had served a number of years in prison only to be exonerated of the alleged crime because, uh, well, he had never actually committed it! Not guilty. Bias became the jury's barrier. They overlooked the evidence. He was innocent and should have never been incarcerated. They had one job: to seriously examine the words of the witnesses and the evidence submitted from both the prosecution and defense. Every jury's aim should be to avoid such a monumental mistake at all costs.

Allowing the evidence to take us wherever it may lead is of the upmost importance. We need to 'be teachable' as opposed to a mind that is closed and a heart which is hardened on any particular issue. Refusing to hear the truth is equivalent to being ignorant of it—where prejudice is both preconceived and partial before a single word has been uttered. The wisdom of God through the king of Israel's pen contends, 'A rebuke goes deeper into one who has understanding than a hundred blows into a fool' (Prov. 17:10). Wow. I want to be that person *who has understanding* and not the one *who refuses to listen* at his own peril, don't you?

That is exactly where we are in this second chapter. A hearing is about to unfold. The judge is presiding over each and every step. He is evaluating the internal and external evidence to be presented, impartially holding both parties to the law, and guiding the jury as to how best to make an informed decision. His instructions are clear and definitive: 'Keep an open mind throughout the trial. Do not make up your mind about what your verdict will be until the end of the trial when you have heard all the evidence.'[1]

Imagine now that we are seated inside this courtroom and have just received his counsel. We are located to the side of the presiding judge, sitting in the jury box. Yup,

---

1. Pennsylvania Supreme Court, *Pennsylvania Suggested Standard Civil Jury Instructions* (Mechanicsburg: PBI Press, 2011), 1.180.

we are the jury. And in this case, we have already been presented with the evidence of the previous chapter.

We now know that the Bible is in fact the very Word of God. This was easy to conclude from the various presentations made to the jury. We had seen the divine activity involved to receive it, the superior claims of its authenticity and accuracy, as well as its inescapable authority. Not a single soul on the jury could deny that it is the very Word of God. The Bible can no longer be disregarded as a mythological book of stories. It is a unified message from God. But can it be said beyond a reasonable doubt that it is the *only* message from God?

That is why we are seated in the jury box. We are charged with the responsibility of deciding, based upon the eyewitness testimony we are about to hear, whether the plantiff's accusation that 'all religions are the same' is a valid one. Is this second statement a half-truth or is it something we need to avow?

When faced with this prospect, that the Bible is one of many good books from a good god, a number of questions naturally arise:

- Can we conclude that at the heart of every religion is the very same god?

- Is there a slew of similarities between each of the world's religions?

- Should we equally value *The Sutras*, *The Quran*, *The Vedas*, and *The Book of Mormon*?

- Does god exist in a garden variety of ways to mankind?

- Is our view of god socially constructed—a projection of

the culture we are raised in?

- Could all of this curiosity be attributed to some psychological need to believe in a god?

If you were to answer 'yes' to any of these questions, then it would not matter which way you proceed in your life, so long as you move towards this god of many religions in some way. Your hope, or the stated outcome of each would lead to something supernaturally similar, right? What would it matter what you believe in, so long as you do believe in *something*? Whether you identify as an Agnostic, Baha'i, Buddhist, Catholic, Christian, Christian Scientist, Free-Mason, Gypsy, Hindu, Jehovah's Witness, Jew, Mormon, Muslim, Rastafarian, Seventh-Day Adventist, Shinto, Sikh, Unitarian Universalist, or a Wiccan (to name just a few)—they would all have to lead and link to an indomitable god, correct?

At least that's the plaintiff's charges. He is making the accusation against Christianity that all religions at their core are one and the same. The accuser is alleging that the God of the Bible is simply a representative form of the god of all mankind; all religions are on an equal footing; and Christians have no right to declare that there is only 'one way' to eternal life with their God.

Will these arguments be sufficient enough to carry the jury? Is the defense attorney able to substantiate—by the most convincing credentials—that these claims are untrue? Is there any validity to the exclusivity of Christianity, a religion based on the Person and works of Jesus Christ? And can it withstand close scrutiny? We will hear from the defense attorney and his witnesses shortly.

THE HALF-TRUTH

ALL RELIGIONS ARE THE SAME.

The claim has been made that the Bible is a good book from a good god, and that it is not the only one. This is the point of contention. Most would agree that Jesus Christ, the focal point of the Bible, was also the centerpiece of human history. After all, His life divides time into two chapters: B.C., 'before Christ' and A.D., Latin for 'in the year of our Lord.'[2] Almost every major religion of man teaches that Jesus was a good teacher (we will examine this in greater detail in chapter four). Yet, this does not mean a pluralist would fully embrace Christ's words, exclusive words such as, 'for unless you believe that I am He, you will die in your sins' (John 8:24).

'All religions are the same' implies an inclusivity, not an exclusivity. It is the idea that all 'truth' is the same god's truth. All of the world's religions are on an equal footing and equally legitimate.

Sure, they would argue that there may be some distinctions, but behind them is a single, massive meta-narrative—a unifying story of a god who is open and accessible to man through many means.

The problem here is that the Bible tells us something utterly different. It goes intentionally against the grain of these all-embracing, all-inclusive claims. God's Word cannot be coalesced with another because it is unlike any

---

2. John MacArthur, *The MacArthur New Testament Commentary, John 12-21* (Chicago: Moody Publishers, 2008), 2.

other. To attempt to reconcile Christianity with the religions of the world is to plead ignorance before the court.

Dr. Sproul recognizes the predicament that these kind of gross overstatements inescapably produce:

> If you really look, in a comparative way, analyzing the content of world religions with each other—a cursory glance will show you that these religions are not the same; and at many points are mutually exclusive. I hear people say, 'there is this underlining unity, we all believe the same thing.' That's not true. What Muslims believe about what is good and the nature of redemption is radically different from what Christianity teaches, for example. Buddha was an atheist who simply claimed to be enlightened, Confucius talked about the veneration of ancestors—that's a long way from the faith of the Scriptures.[3]

No one wants to sound foolish. However, that's exactly what happens when a person attempts to assert that these religions are all equally valid. Sproul simplifies, rather astutely, the impossibility of such a declaration:

> And what you don't have in Buddhism and Islam, Confucianism, Shintoism, Taoism, and these other religions is an atonement. You don't have a way of redemption that we have in Christianity, nor do you have a living Mediator. Moses is dead, Buddha is dead, Confucius is dead, and Muhammad is dead. There is no resurrection in these other religions. Christianity has elements to it, content to it, that distinguish it from all other religions, and with that

---

3. R.C. Sproul, *Defending Your Faith* teaching series: Lecture 32 "Questions and Answers." https://www.ligonier.org/learn/series/defending-your-faith/

distinction comes the claim of Christ that it is the only true way to God.[4]

Re-read the last sentence from Sproul, as it is pregnant with meaning. In effect, he is saying they have no case. They are literally poles apart, with irreconcilable views and incompatible objectives. The prosecution's argument 'all religions are the same' is really nothing more than a brand of arrogance in disguise. A verbal flame thrower! To stand behind this half-truth is to take the easy way out, hoping that all those who hear it will be undiscerning and unprepared to respond to such a challenge. And it is a good wager, as many will do just that—and fall prey to such an absurd allegation.

In this chapter, we get to hear from the defense, led by an elder statesman of the church, the apostle John.[5] As a member of Jesus' most intimate circle, John is supremely qualified to honestly and accurately present the facts. He rightly knows the claims of Christianity because he was there with Christ. But this case is not about himself. Perhaps that is why he never mentions his own name in the entire Gospel account. (The only 'John' ever mentioned by name is 'John the Baptist.') John's focus is a singular One and he points to the purpose of his tome (the Gospel of John) in 20:31. It is for all to see and believe 'that Jesus is the

---

4. Ibid.

5. You can learn more about the apostle John (and the other eleven men who were chosen as Christ's disciples) by reading John MacArthur's *Twelve Ordinary Men* (Nashville: W Publishing Group, 2002). It was John who referred to himself in his Gospel account as 'the disciple whom Jesus loved' (cf. 13:23). 110.

Christ' and thereby 'have life in His Name.'[6] Christianity in a nutshell.

And so he has the burden of proof—a number of witnesses scheduled to testify in direct opposition to the false religions of man. We, the jury, must listen intently to those being called to the stand. They have each affirmed the testimony they are about to give before the court as 'the truth, the whole truth, and nothing but the truth, so help me God.'

If you are willing to read on, that is exactly what you will discover. The Gospel of John is a record of a court hearing that every living soul should read and carefully consider as to its truthfulness. The heart of mankind is weighing in the balance.

THE WHOLE TRUTH

*ALL RELIGIONS ARE THE SAME, **EXCEPT CHRISTIANITY.***

On this day, the courtroom's gallery is full-to-overflowing. The judge hammers his gavel three times to quiet the room and the hum of voices begin to fall silent. He has everyone's undivided attention. 'You may begin your defense, counselor.' It is official, court is back in session. John rises from his seat behind one of two small tables located in front of the judge's bench. The prosecution is seated at the other one. All eyes are upon the apostle as John knows that he must convince us, the jury, of the prosecution's claim as a half-truth.

---

6. R.C. Sproul, *St. Andrew's Expositional Commentary on John*, (Lake Mary: Reformation Trust Publishing, 2009), 394.

The apostle begins his opening statement to all within listening distance. His convictions are running deep. John is a man committed to the whole truth—not just to empty platitudes used to elicit emotions. His rebuttal to the prosecution's argument will be that all religions are not the same, that there is one which stands apart from all the others. But in order for John to demonstrate this, the jury will need to hear from the strongest and most solid witnesses ever to enter a courtroom; and indeed, they are. These accounts, on their own merit, corroborate the transcript from the highest court in all of human history. What we will be reading from is John's Gospel, and in it four witnesses (John the Baptist, the works of Christ, God the Father, and the Scriptures) have given testimony to the exclusiveness of Christianity. Picture each of them ready to take the stand in this courtroom. But first, John must address the judge and jury. He does so with this text—the words of Christ:

> If I alone testify about Myself, My testimony is not true. There is another who testifies of Me, and I know that the testimony which He gives about Me is true. You have sent to *John* [the Baptist], and he has testified to the truth. But the testimony which I receive is not from man, but I say these things so that you may be saved. He was the lamp that was burning and was shining and you were willing to rejoice for a while in his light. But the testimony which I have is greater than the testimony of John [the Baptist]; for *the works* which the Father has given Me to accomplish—the very works that I do—testify about Me, that the Father has sent Me. And *the Father* who sent Me, He has testified of Me. You have neither heard His voice at any time nor seen His form. You do not have His word abiding in you,

for you do not believe Him whom He sent. You search *the Scriptures* because you think that in them you have eternal life; it is these that testify about Me; and you are unwilling to come to Me so that you may have life (John 5:31-40, emphasis mine).

THE WITNESS OF JOHN THE BAPTIST

The first person the apostle calls to the witness stand is a man familiar to many. He is the messenger known as 'John the Baptist.' Contrary to his name, John the Baptist did much more than baptize. He was a faithful forerunner to the Messiah. This was the prophet used by God as a witness to announce the coming of God's Son Jesus Christ. The apostle summarizes the role of this outspoken ambassador, stating,

There came a man sent from God, whose name was John. He came as a *witness*, to testify about the Light, so that all might believe through him. He was not the Light, but he came to testify about the Light. (John 1:6-9, emphasis mine).

It should be noted that John's Gospel can be read in its entirety in roughly two hours. (This is time well-spent.) If you were to do so, you would find the word 'witness' appearing quite often. In fact, it is used fourteen times as a noun, and another thirty-three times as a verb.[7] Combined and compared, these forms only appear a total of six times in the other Gospel accounts (Matthew, Mark, and Luke). Merrill C. Tenney notes that '[the] Johannine usages of these two terms outnumber their total usage in the rest of the New

---

7. μαρτυρία and μαρτυρέω respectively.

Testament.'[8] John is intentionally using the concept of the witness to point people firsthand to the whole truth. An eye-witness will help to separate fact from fiction. Tenney adds that the first use of this concept of a 'witness' in 1:7 is 'closely related to the progressive presentation of the person of Jesus in the Johannine narrative … John [the Baptist] was the messenger who directed men's faith toward God, not the object of faith himself.'[9]

John the Baptist was a selfless man, and here he serves as the first witness on the stand. His words bridge the Old and New Testament together. He visibly and faithfully served as the forerunner to Jesus Christ. John the Baptist proclaimed the promised Messiah ('the chosen One,' Mal. 3:1), introduced Immanuel ('God with us,' Matt. 1:23), and looked to the living Logos ('the Word of God,' John 1:14). It was his life's mission to be God's messenger. He had one purpose, to tell others about the saving Son of God—which is the exclusive claim of Christianity.

At one time, John the Baptist's ministry had become so popular that some thought him to be the Messiah! Yet, he never claimed to be God himself. His magnificent testimony repeatedly denied his own Messiahship. 'And he confessed and did not deny, but confessed, "I am not the Christ"' (John 1:20). This is seen again in 3:28, 'You yourselves are my witnesses that I said, "I am not the Christ," but, "I have been sent ahead of Him."' There's no question in the courtroom that John the Baptist viewed Jesus Christ as the superior One sent from God. Further testimony is given in 1:30, 'This

8. Merrill C. Tenney, 'Topics from the Gospel of John, Part III: The Meaning of "Witness" in John', *Bibliotheca Sacra* (July 1975), 229.

9. Ibid, 230.

is He on behalf of whom I said, "After me comes a Man who has a higher rank than I, for He existed before me."'

THE WITNESS OF CHRIST AND HIS WORKS

The second person called to the witness stand by the apostle John is Jesus Christ Himself. This made sense, and many had expected it, since John the Baptist was continually making reference to Him under oath. However, in a startling move before the court, Christ declined to be His own witness. He knew full well that the Pharisees and Sadducees would reject it formally, raising an objection based upon the Old Testament Law. Christ's testimony would not be fully admissible according to Deuteronomy 19:15, which stated that 'on the evidence of two or three witnesses a matter shall be confirmed.' Those witnesses would need to be someone other than the individual who is on trial. With Christ as the dominant theme of Christianity, the judge would likely sustain their objection, meaning Christ would not be able to testify on His own behalf.

Jesus knew this, but was not discounting His own testimony by His refusal to testify. As the Son of God, every word Jesus speaks is truth—God's truth. He stood and told the court, 'Even if I testify about Myself, My testimony is true' (John 8:14).

Much like a clever chess player, the apostle John pointed the jury to the works of Christ instead of His words. Move by move, John began to share with his audience miracle after miracle. He began first with Jesus having turned water into wine at the wedding in Cana of Galilee (2:9). He then spoke of Nicodemus, a ruler of the Pharisees, who had shared that it was the works of Christ which caught His very own attention (3:1-2). This was followed by a Samaritan woman at a well declaring that only the Son of God could know her secret sins (4:29). Jesus was also identified as the One healing a royal official's son (4:51), feeding five thousand people in the northern region of Galilee (6:2, 11), walking on water (6:19), and healing a man who was born blind (9:6-7).

And as if that was not enough, John then deftly described the resurrection of a close personal friend, the infamous Lazarus. He had been raised from the dead by the power of Jesus' words, 'Lazarus, come forth' (11:43). Some of the disciples originally misunderstood the news that Lazarus had 'fallen asleep ... they thought that He was speaking of literal sleep. So Jesus then said to them plainly, "Lazarus is dead"' (vv. 13-14). Even the prosecution knew there was no need to cross-examine, for he had spent four days decomposing in the grave. Lazarus was a decaying dead man who had been brought back to life by Christ (11:1-44).

But John had something even more miraculous for the court to hear before finishing with the witness of Christ's wondrous works. You see, sharing the details of Lazarus' resurrection with the jury was a mere preview to the most magnificent miracle of all—the resurrection of Jesus Christ. He, Himself, rose from the dead after having been crucified and sealed in a tomb for three days (20:9). There would be no greater display of Christ's works than His very own resurrection. It was irrefutable testimony. Moreover, the risen Christ of Christianity had appeared to the disciples at the Sea of Galilee (21:6).

With that, the apostle John dismissed his witness simply out of concern for the court's time, stating, 'there are also many other things which Jesus did, which if they were written in detail, I suppose that even the world itself would not contain the books that would be written' (21:25). The evidence was massive and mounting. John could have stopped here and it would have been enough for the jury to render a verdict. But he didn't …

THE WITNESS OF GOD THE FATHER

The third person the apostle decided to call to the witness stand was none other than God the Father. John MacArthur has written that this testimony 'is of infinitely greater importance than any human testimony.'[10] The Creator, the Almighty, the Majestic Glory, is the greatest Witness any mortal man could have. This is *the* Sovereign LORD of the universe. The One called Yahweh, who told Moses at the burning bush, 'I AM WHO I AM' (Exod. 3:14).

You could hear a pin drop when His Name was spoken in the courtroom.

John went on to explain that it is God the Father who has directly and definitively testified to the exclusive claims of Christ. The Father did this twice early in Jesus' ministry. First, during His baptism in Matthew 3:17, we read, 'and behold, a voice out of the heavens said, "This is My beloved Son, in whom I am well-pleased."' Second, at an event known as 'the transfiguration.' Matthew 17:5 reads, 'behold, a voice out of the cloud said, "This is My beloved Son, with whom I am well-pleased; listen to Him!"'[11]

---

10. MacArthur, *The MacArthur New Testament Commentary, John 12-21,* 212.

11. Both the baptism of Jesus (specifically, the Father's words) and the transfiguration are not recorded in the Gospel of John, but rather in all three Synoptic (meaning similar) Gospels (Matt. 3:13–17; Mark 1:9–11; Luke 3:21–22).

Another instance of the Father's affirmation took place when His Son's mission on earth was coming to a close. Jesus would suffer unjustly as no man had ever before; and He would die one of the cruelest deaths ever devised—by means of crucifixion. As one scholar wrote,

> *Crucifixion was a vulgar, common execution that the Romans imposed on notorious criminals, prisoners of war, and rebellious slaves. Its harsh brutality symbolized the supremacy of the Roman government over the victim. Gentiles thus viewed crucifixion as a sure sign of the victim's defeat. Jews, on the other hand, held crucified men in even greater contempt because to them crucifixion was a sign of God's curse on the victim…*
>
> *When Jesus Christ commissioned His disciples to preach the gospel, He sent them with a message that collided with the cultural sensibilities of the day. His death and resurrection were the basis for the forgiveness of sin, yet both Jews and Gentiles found the manner of His death—crucifixion—to be a severe impediment to receiving the gospel because they viewed crucified men with complete disdain.*[12]

The disciples would need some reassurance of Christ's identity. This was not the outcome they had longed for. Their understanding of an 'earthly kingdom to come' leaned heavily upon the present-day and lightly on the latter 'to come.' They expected an earthly takeover that would result in a removal of Rome's rule. Quickly and swiftly. Needless to say, the crucifixion of Christ collided with their calculations. Their world was unraveling right before their eyes.

---

12. Donald E. Green, 'The Folly of the Cross', *The Master's Seminary Journal*, 15/1 (Spring 2004), 59.

The disciples heard Jesus speak often on how these events were orchestrated and ordained by *El Elyon* ('God Most High'). The Son had often referred back to His Abba Father. In each instance, Jesus was seeking to glorify Him:

> Jesus gave them this answer: 'Very truly I tell you, the Son can do nothing by Himself; He can do only what He sees His Father doing, because whatever the Father does the Son also does' (5:19 NIV).

> My teaching is not My own. It comes from the One who sent Me (7:16 NIV).

> I have much to say in judgment of you. But He who sent Me is trustworthy, and what I have heard from Him I tell the world (8:26).

> So Jesus said, 'When you have lifted up the Son of Man, then you will know that I am He and that I do nothing on My own but speak just what the Father has taught Me' (8:28 NIV).

Again, the Son of God desired that the Father would be glorified. This was John's main point and he would not let up. He was leading the jury down a path that would cause them to hear the greatest possible declaration. Soon, this selfless and sinless act of substitution by the Son would prompt the Father to speak.

John continued, describing (in his Gospel) the time—just prior to the crucifixion—when Jesus had been praying to His Father. The Son's desire was for Him to receive the glory from what would take place at the cross. And it happened.

It was at this moment, John shared, when a voice from heaven gave witness to the One who would fulfill such a costly commission:

> 'Now is my soul troubled. And what shall I say? "Father, save me from this hour"? But for this purpose I have come to this hour. Father, glorify your Name.' Then a voice came from heaven: 'I have glorified it, and I will glorify it again' (12:27-28 ESV).[13]

God the Father, by answering Christ's glory-request, was giving witness to the fulfillment of Old Testament prophecy concerning the Messiah in this trial—a first-hand account by the Eternal One that Jesus Christ was the chosen One.[14]

We have just heard riveting testimony! It seemed at this point that the confirmation of Christianity's exclusivity could not be stronger. Perhaps it was time for John to 'rest his case.' And he might have done so, except for the divine dialogue that was about to follow.

THE WITNESS OF THE SCRIPTURE

The final witness called to the stand by John was the very Word of God. The accused is usually the last to take the stand for the defense—and it would be no different in this trial. John would briefly bring the jury back to the crime scene, where it all started.

English theologian A. W. Pink once remarked, 'Upon the foundation of divine inspiration of the Bible stands or falls

---

13. God's voice was heard by the 'crowd of people who stood there' (12:29). However, they attempted to explain it away by attributing it to the sound of thunder or even an angel speaking.

14. It was the fulfillment of these prophetic words in Isaiah 42:1, 'Behold, My Servant, whom I uphold; My chosen One in whom My soul delights.'

the entire edifice of Christian truth … It is useless to discuss any doctrine taught by the Bible until you are prepared to acknowledge, unreservedly, that the Bible is the final court of appeal.'[15] The exclusivity of Christianity rests on the exclusive Word of God and its exclusive claims of Christ.

As was read earlier from 5:39, John had quoted Jesus as saying, 'You search the Scriptures because you think that in them you have eternal life; it is these that testify about Me.' He adds later in verse 46, 'For if you believed Moses, you would believe Me, for he wrote about Me.'

The son of a lawyer, reformer John Calvin once wrote, 'By *the Scriptures,* it is well known… [to mean] the Old Testament; for it was not in the Gospel that Christ first began to be manifested, but having received testimony from the Law and the Prophets, he was openly exhibited in the Gospel.'[16] The Old and New Testaments are just that, testimonies to the exclusivity of Christianity. The Bible provides the perfect proof. As exclusive evidence it answers with arresting authority. There can be no other religion, no additional holy books, and no ambiguous god.

This was more than enough. The witness was asked by the presiding judge to step down. He excused the jury, knowing that they would require some time of deliberation behind closed doors. Upon their return an inquiry would have to be made from the bench. Only one ultimate question would remain: 'Has the jury reached a verdict?'

---

15. A.W. Pink, *The Divine Inspiration of the Bible* (Swengel: Bible Truth Depot, 1917), 2.

16. John Calvin, *Calvin's Commentaries: Volume XVII* (Grand Rapids: Baker Books, 2009), 218.

WHOLE MEANING

The purpose of a witness is to persuade. A witness is used to verify whether the claim that is being made is truthful. John understood this and produced several eyewitnesses throughout his Gospel account. There were four testimonies from John 5:31-40 highlighted in this chapter (John the Baptist, God the Father, Christ and His Works, and the Scriptures), but they are not the only ones to be found in the Gospel of John.

The apostle references the Holy Spirit as He descends like a dove to supernaturally affirm the Son of God (1:32), and later tells of a blind man who scolded others for not recognizing nor believing the supernatural claims of Christ. We read, 'The man answered and said to them, "Well, here is an amazing thing, that you do not know where He is from, and yet He opened my eyes"' (9:30).

A 'witness' word study yields even more fruitful testimony. For example, the Trinity (Father, Son, and Holy Spirit) bears witness to the identity of Christ. Jesus speaks of His *Father's* testimony when He says, 'I am He who testifies about Myself, and the Father who sent Me testifies about Me' (8:18). Jesus also speaks of the *Holy Spirit's* witness, 'He will glorify Me, for He will take of Mine and will disclose it to you' (16:14). When addressing Pilate, Christ declared of *Himself,* 'You say correctly that I am a king. For this I have been born, and for this I have come into the world, to testify to the truth. Everyone who is of the truth hears My voice' (18:37).

Lastly, the apostle and author John serves as the final witness as he closes His Gospel. He writes, 'This is the disciple who is testifying to these things and wrote these things, and we know that his testimony is true' (21:24). The entire Gospel of John serves as an accurate narration, a faithful testimony, a truth-telling witness. 'And he who has seen has testified, and his testimony is true; and he knows that he is telling the truth, so that you also may believe' (19:35).

There can be no doubt of the author's intended thematic use of witnesses throughout the Gospel of John. Nor can there be any question as to how powerfully and persuasively they each declare the exclusive claim of Christianity—that Jesus Christ is the Son of God. The evidence was laid out before John's original audience, and has since been recorded for generations to examine.

In the last chapter we looked at the activity, authenticity, and authority of Scripture. This one had much to do with its application. Have you reached a verdict? Do you believe the half-truth: All religions are the same, or the whole truth: all religions are the same, *except Christianity*? If Puritan J.C. Ryle were in the juror's box with you, here is what he would have said about those who still hold to the half-truth, 'Hard must those hearts have been which could hear such testimony, and yet remain unmoved!'[17]

SUMMARY

- **The Half-Truth:** it is a claim that all religions are basically the same—ultimately leading us to a similar supernatural something. This statement alleges that the God of the Bible is simply a representative form of this god of all mankind; all religions are on an equal footing; and Christians have no right to declare that

---

17. J.C. Ryle, *Expository Thoughts on John*. Volume 1 (Carlisle: Banner of Truth, 2012), 211.

there is only 'one way' to eternal life through Jesus Christ.

- **The Whole-Truth:** all religions are the same, *except Christianity*. Before the court we have heard 'the truth, the whole truth, and nothing but the truth, so help me, God.' Four witnesses, John the Baptist, the works of Christ, God the Father, and the Scriptures gave testimony to the exclusivity of Jesus Christ and Christianity.

- **The Whole Meaning:** these accounts from the Gospel of John corroborate the transcript from the highest court in all of human history. God's Word cannot be coalesced with another because it is unlike any other. One cannot reconcile Christianity with the religions of the world as it would have to come at the cost of truth.

3.
HALF-TRUTH #3:
GOD IS LOVE

CONCERNING GOD

Gay. Fundamentalist. Minion. These words are in frequent use today—and yet, their meanings have radically changed over the course of time. Each one has experienced a semantic shift. Their interpretations, as defined by our culture, are altogether different from what was originally intended.

Take the word 'gay.' At first, it was known as an adjective portraying someone or thing as merry and carefree (i.e., 'don we now our gay apparel').[1] This festive expression then

---

1. English Oxford Living Dictionaries. https://en.oxforddictionaries.com/definition/gay. The website also notes under the heading usage, 'Gay meaning "homosexual" became established in the 1960s as the term preferred by homosexual men to describe themselves. It is now the standard accepted term throughout the English-speaking world. As a result, the centuries-old other senses of gay meaning either "carefree" or "bright and showy" have more or less dropped out of natural use. The word gay cannot be readily used today in these older senses without arousing

transitioned into a negative term to describe something as 'foolish, stupid, or unimpressive.'[2] Today, you and I both know this word as a common noun; an identifier for a man who is homosexual.[3]

Another example of this progression is seen with 'fundamentalist.' At one time, its usage was a 'direct reaction to the increasing influence of "liberal" or "modernist" forms of Christianity.'[4]

To say you were a 'fundamentalist' would mean that you had identified with the fundamentals of the Christian faith. Basically, you were a Bible-believing, gospel-giving, conservative-living Christian who held to its core creeds. This is no longer the case, as Phil Johnson explains:[5]

> Look, there are certain doctrines that are so basic, so fundamental, that if you deny them, or if you do away with them, then you've really undermined the whole basis for the Christian faith. These are the fundamentals of the faith. I believe there are doctrines that are that important. And in that sense, my heart beats with the

a sense of double entendre, despite concerted attempts by some to keep them alive. Gay in its modern sense typically refers to men (lesbian being the standard term for homosexual women) but in some contexts it can be used of both men and women.' The word 'queer' has also undergone a similar metamorphosis.

2. Ibid. Often employed both offensively and informally, i.e., 'That song is so gay!'

3. *Merriam-Webster.* https://www.merriam-webster.com/dictionary/gay.

4. Stanley J. Grenz, David Guretzki, Cherith Fee Nordling, *Pocket Dictionary of Theological Terms* (Downers Grove: InterVarsity Press, 1999), 54.

5. Taken from an interview on *Rightly Divided with Lane Chaplin: Defining and Defending Historic Evangelicalism with guest Phil Johnson,* https://www.youtube.com/watch?v=O8NTmQZLbY4 (October 25, 2009). Phil Johnson is the executive director of *Grace to You,* and a pastor/elder at Grace Community Church in Sun Valley, CA.

original fundamentalists, and what people meant by that word when the name was coined. But it doesn't mean the same thing anymore. Now a fundamentalist is a radical Muslim with a bomb … I wouldn't call yourself that today, especially if you are about to get on an airplane.

He's right! Much of our discourse from years past has been hollowed-out. Informed by an ever-changing culture, our language is being linguistically contorted. It is a blatant attempt to reinvent reality. We have a moral imagination, which makes it hard to stay current, to keep up—as a number of our English words and phrases have become obsolete. They are linked elsewhere; and take on a new ethos. They identify with something that is in conflict with its previous (and often defunct) meaning. Even the slave-driving word 'minion' has been altered from an undignified peon to those loveable little yellow guys in the *Despicable Me* series.[6]

We like to play with our words:

- If you are told to 'swipe' at something, you will undoubtedly do this with a smart phone and an index finger.

- If you state that something is 'awful,' it did not fill you with awe. Just the opposite, you found it to be quite appalling.

- If you were to receive some 'spam,' you will most likely desire to delete it—not eat it.

---

6. Who wouldn't want one of Gru's minions? With just a crack and a shake, these little guys double as glow sticks! See http://despicableme.wikia. com/wiki/Minions.

- If you plan to use your 'cell,' there is no need to purchase a powerful electron microscope in order to isolate one. However, you will require a strong signal.

- If you are labeled by others as an 'egghead,' it is not because you have a shaved head. Instead, you decided to use it.

Hysterical, yes?[7] Here are a few more to think on: 'dope,' 'virus,' 'weed,' 'troll,' 'über,' and 'wicked.' These words, along with many others, all suffer from the same symptoms. Call it a cultural amnesia where we intentionally forget the origin, and then alter it to reflect a new attitude or innovation. The list of words and phrases caught in this semantic drift will inevitably lengthen during any technological or moral revolution; and we just so happen to be alive in both.

Sadly, God's character has undergone this same kind of semantic abuse, especially as it relates to His affection towards mankind. 'God is love' is an all-important phrase that has been sanitized and sentimentalized over recent years—representing only what the culture is morally comfortable with. This condition can be diagnosed as an allergy towards authority.

Counsel is now given for us to live as we would desire to live—guilt-free and shame-free. Our problem, as some argue, is not with God's love, but with a need for us to love ourselves just as we are. 'Do whatever makes *you* happy, whatever *feels* right.' Sounds a bit selfish? It should, it's a passion play. A call to let self (and sin) take its course, all under the guise of God's love. And it sounds something like

---

7. As in 'comical'; I was not referring to a moment of delirium and disorientation. Again, it is a matter of semantics.

this, 'We need to stay true to what's on the inside. I mean, doesn't the Bible say that "God is love"?'

Yes, it does. You will find no dispute from believers and unbelievers alike—the phrase was birthed from Scripture. It definitely declares this attribute: 'God is love' (1 John 4:8).[8] But does God's love leave any room for His justice and wrath? There are many who adamantly argue that the loving God of the New Testament is incompatible with the vengeful One of the Old.[9] Perhaps you have heard it said before that 'a loving God isn't a judging One.' Or, to put it another way, 'If God is a God of love, then how could He send anyone to hell?'

What did the apostle John mean when he maintained in the Bible that 'God is love'? It is imperative that we recognize the right meaning and reject the wrong ones attributed to this text. If our view of Him has been guided by emotion, then we need to know that it may be in error. Twentieth century theologian A.W. Tozer expressed the same concern:[10]

What comes into our minds when we think about God, is the most important thing about us. Worship is pure or base—as the worshiper entertains high or low thoughts of God. For this reason the gravest question before the Church is always God Himself, and the most portentous fact about

---

8. He is also called 'The God of love' in 2 Corinthians 13:11.

9. An Old Testament text referencing God's hatred of those who rebel is Psalm 11:5, 'The LORD tests the righteous and the wicked, and the one who loves violence His soul hates.' Another is found in Hosea 9:15, 'All their evil is at Gilgal; indeed, I came to hate them there! Because of the wickedness of their deeds I will drive them out of My house! I will love them no more; all their princes are rebels.'

10. A.W. Tozer, *The Knowledge of the Holy* (New York: HarperCollins, 1978), 1.

any man is not what he at a given time may say or do—but what he in his deep heart conceives God to be like. It is impossible to keep our moral practices sound and our inward attitudes right, while our idea of God is erroneous or inadequate. No religion has ever been greater than its idea of God. Worship is pure or base—as the worshiper entertains high or low thoughts of God. We tend by a secret law of the soul, to move toward our mental image of God … Were we able to extract from any man a complete answer to the question, 'What comes into your mind when you think about God?' we might predict with certainty the spiritual future of that man … A right conception of God is basic not only to correct theology, but to practical Christian living as well. There is scarcely an error in doctrine, or a failure in applying Christian ethics—that cannot be traced finally to false and ignoble thoughts about God.

As we have already established in previous chapters, these truths must arise from *the* Truth—we can go to no other source than the authoritative Word of God to learn about God. It is the prescribed immunotherapy for this kind of allergy. What we affirm about God cannot be subject to the whims of modern love, for there is a direct correlation between our understanding of God and how we choose to live. Your knowledge of Him is foundational to everything you think, say, and do. A low (or erroneous) view will always degenerate into godlessness, whereas a high (or biblical) view can only engender godliness.[11]

Brace yourself, because this really matters.

---

11. The apostle Paul opened with this practical principle in his letter to Titus, emphasizing that it is a 'knowledge of the truth that leads to godliness' (1:1, NIV).

THE HALF-TRUTH

GOD IS LOVE.

This is the only attribute that some will ever choose to believe about God. Albeit, it is an altered one, where our Creator is looking down upon His planet earth with an unconditional affection towards everyone. It sounds so good, so non-threatening, and so peace-loving, so why poke at it?

Because the endearing expression has been hijacked from the Bible and bubble-wrapped to make the Almighty not so mighty. As the mantra goes, 'God loves me just as I am.' We need to see this interpretation for what it really is: smugness; a self-centered, individualistic view which disregards the fall of man, and dilutes God's constitution into something unbiblical and ineffectual. It has become a form of philosophy that perverts the nature of God for the sake of one's own personal pleasure.

In reality, this sentiment has become yet another victim of semantics—and its result is a new half-truth. Something has been revealed and concealed. Consciously and unconsciously, this phrase has been spoken to distance oneself away from moral accountability. And, for the most part, the move remains undetected. People buy it in large quantities. There are no penalty clauses, and no contractual obligations. There is only a cultural call to be tolerant of seemingly everything except the phrase's original meaning.

Distorting the love of God[12] points to a seismic change in our contemporary culture—one that erroneously alters the

---

12. This phrase was taken from the title of a lecture given by D.A. Carson at Dallas Theological Seminary, *On Distorting the Love God*, January 5, 1998. The thirty minute chapel message (the first of four theological discourses)

posture of God towards the unrepentant, thereby rejecting the biblical teaching of a literal and eternal hell. Not only does this half-truth imply a person is exempt from the moral Law, but it also intimates that God's holy nature has been seriously exaggerated. Yes, we most certainly agree that 'God is love,' but not at the expense of His holiness. What is missing is the non-contradictory truth of the whole of Scripture as it relates to the character of God.

Words, phrases, and their meanings all matter.

Remember, the slippery slide of semantics degrades the meaning of any word (or in this case, a phrase) into something utterly unlike its original. In a lecture given to the students and faculty of Dallas Theological Seminary, D.A. Carson described the challenge this presents:

> If people believe in god at all today, the overwhelming majority hold that this 'god,' however he, she, or it may be understood, is a loving being. But that is what makes the task of the Christian witness so daunting. For this widely disseminated belief in 'the love of God' is set with increasing frequency in some matrix other than biblical theology. The result is that when informed Christians talk about 'the love of God' they mean something very different from what is meant in the surrounding culture. Worse, neither side may perceive that this is the case … to put this another way, in present-day Western culture many other and complementary truths about God are widely disbelieved. I do not think that what the Bible says about the love of God can long survive at the forefront of our thinking if it is abstracted from the sovereignty of God,

can be found online at http://www.dts.edu/media/play/on-distorting-the-love-of-god-d-a-carson/.

the holiness of God, the wrath of God, the providence of God, the personhood of God, to mention only a few nonnegotiable elements of basic Christianity.[13]

To Dr. Carson's point, this half-truth seeks to defang the biblical character of God by taking the terror out of it. What are we to do with the New Testament declaration that '[i]t is a terrifying thing to fall into the hands of the living God' (Heb. 10:31)? I would contend that a biblical worldview on the love of God has been replaced with a secular one. In a sense, man has attempted to air-condition hell.

THE WHOLE TRUTH

GOD IS LOVE AND HOLY, HOLY, HOLY.

Scripture most definitely supports the certitude that God is love. His unconditional care and concern, without question, extends to each-and-everyone. In its most simplified form, we see God's love on display in the world we live in. Ever since the dawn of His creation God has been intrinsically known by the entirety of mankind. The breath-taking handiwork of the Creator can be effortlessly perceived. What I mean to say here is that it is impossible for a human being to miss this reality. Yes, there are people who suppress it all the time—even ignore it. But no one is truly able to make the claim of an atheist—pleading ignorance about God's existence and nature—as the evidence is all around us. It is so 'clearly seen' that we are without an excuse in this regard to recognize it.[14]

---

13. Ibid.

14. 'For since the creation of the world His invisible attributes, His eternal power and divine nature, have been clearly seen, being understood

Furthermore, did you know that you are a recipient of His love? All of mankind has been given such a gift. Irrespective of your acknowledgment of a divine Creator, His providential care reaches you, affects you, impacts you. Each of us, in some manner, are beneficiaries of the love of God. His favor, in this regard, is extended to all. Psalm 145:9 (NIV) declares that the 'LORD is good to all; He has compassion on all He has made.'

COMMON GRACE

Theologically speaking, this is what is known as the doctrine of common grace. It is 'common' in that it touches every man, woman, and child; 'grace' in that it is not deserved, earned, or merited. Dr. Heath Lambert in his book *A Theology of Biblical Counseling* supplies us with a helpful definition:

> Common grace is the good kindness of God that He shows to all people regardless of whether they have experienced the salvation that comes through Jesus Christ alone. It is called common because it comes to all people—believers and unbelievers alike. It is referred to as grace because this kindness is undeserved. People are born in sin and so do not deserve any blessing from God, only judgment. That God would allow people to live and to experience many blessings of life is a great kindness… One of the clearest places we see this in the Bible is in Matthew 5:43-45: 'You have heard that it was said, 'You shall love your neighbor and hate your enemy.' But I say to you, love your enemies and pray for those who persecute you, so that you may

through what has been made, so that they are without excuse' (Rom. 1:20). While they may 'suppress the truth in unrighteousness' (v. 18), every man knows that there is a God. That knowledge is within all people, 'because God has made it plain to them' (v. 19).

be sons of your Father who is in heaven; *for He causes His sun to rise on the evil and the good, and sends rain on the righteous and the unrighteous.*'[15]

Another confirmation of His common grace is seen in our 'intellectual life'[16] where God has given humankind intellect and innovation. Many of us can be thankful for our safe surroundings, where we have medical and technological advancements that improve upon our lives daily. Imagine what your days would be like without cell phones, electricity, hospitals, and running water. Again, God is love.

His common grace physically and intellectually is unquestionably true. Common—bestowing blessings to all, and grace—not a single soul deserves it, nor can make any claim to it. But for a person to assert that this is the *only* kind of love that exists from God, with little or no regard for the whole truth, is reckless (another half-truth, for sure).

SAVING GRACE

Like two sides of the same coin, God's love not only includes a *common grace* for all mankind indiscriminately, but also a *saving grace* specifically for those who come to faith in Christ. This greater love results in a soul being saved from eternal death and hell. The apostle Paul wrote in his letter to the church of Ephesus about God's '*great love* with which

---

15. Heath Lambert, *A Theology of Biblical Counseling: The Doctrinal Foundations of Counseling Ministry* (Grand Rapids: Zondervan, 2016), 67-68. Emphasis mine. Dr. Lambert adds, 'Jesus urges His hearers to be like God in being kind to people who hate them. The point He makes is that God is kind to all by sending the sun and rain to all people, believers and unbelievers alike. You do not have to be saved to enjoy the sun at the beach or to have crops watered. God sends those blessings to everyone.'

16. I have borrowed this phrase from Dr. Lambert, *A Theology of Biblical Counseling*. 69.

He loved us,' explaining to them that 'by *grace* you have been *saved* through *faith*.'[17] Believers have been saved from God, from facing God's righteous judgment of sin.

God's saving love is so much more than common, and to describe it as such is to lack the biblical knowledge about His perfections as He has revealed them to us.

Only the Word of God will inoculate a person from such heresy. We must consider the full array of God's love as it is presented in the Bible. The whole truth equates to possessing a right understanding of God. When rooted in Scripture, our thinking on the love of God will move us from the shallow end to the deep end of the pool. John MacArthur explains:

> The love of God … is a pure and holy love, consistent with all other divine attributes … The simple statement 'God is love' obviously does not convey everything that can be known about God. We know from Scripture that He is also holy and righteous and true to His Word. God's love does not contradict His holiness; instead, it complements and magnifies it and gives it its deepest meaning. So we cannot isolate this one phrase from the rest of Scripture and attempt to make love represent the sum of what we know about God. [18]

Semantics has no sway on Scripture. The culture cannot change this phrase's meaning. 'God is love'—but it is a *holy love*. It is a love that infuses and permeates the entire

---

17. Ephesians 2:4b, 8a (emphasis mine). We will explore one's 'faith' with greater specificity in chapter five.

18. John MacArthur, *The Love of God: He Will Do Whatever It Takes to Make Us Holy* (Dallas: Word Publishing, 1996), 28.

character of God. His love and holiness are not mutually exclusive attributes. They co-exist, work in tandem, influencing one another. The whole truth is that God is love *and* holy, holy, holy. While He is affectionate towards us, this does not include an acceptance of our sin. To say it another way: God has a loving holiness. MacArthur adds:

> [W]e know that God is holy, 'undefiled, separated from sinners and exalted above the heavens' (Heb. 7:26). As a holy being, He would be perfectly righteous to view all sinners with the utmost contempt. But His is a loving holiness that reaches out to sinners with salvation for them—the antithesis of aloofness or indifference.[19]

Common grace is seen in God's concern for the general welfare of man—an 'extension of God's favor to all people through providential care, regardless of whether or not they acknowledge and love God.'[20] But it is in His saving grace where God's loving holiness is best understood. The Son of God was sent on a rescue mission to save repentant sinners from the wrath of the Father. There is deliverance from God's punishment of sin found at the cross of Calvary. This love, this grace, has been called amazing, and rightly so.[21]

Saving grace is a gift to be received, not earned. And when it is opened, the genuine believer finds God's

---

19. Ibid, 29.

20. Grenz, Guretzki, and Nordling, *Pocket Dictionary of Theological Terms,* 56.

21. 'Amazing grace' and 'amazing love,' taken from two theologically rich hymns. *Amazing Grace! How Sweet the Sound* ('that saved a wretch like me!'); also, *And Can It Be* ('that I should gain an interest in the Savior's blood?... Amazing love!'). Both are found in *Hymns of Grace* (Los Angeles: The Master's Seminary Press, 2015), 89, 180.

everlasting forgiveness and mercy inside. It can never, ever be taken back by the Giver. There is no expiration date. Its shelf-life will last throughout all eternity. This is an endless kind of love, which comes to us at the greatest expense, from the greatest commodity in the known universe: the blood of Jesus Christ, the Son of God. For all who believe, this free gift was given and will be received. A saving gift known as saving grace.

At the age of twenty-one, C.H. Spurgeon preached a sermon entitled 'A Visit to Calvary.' In it he masterfully illustrated the difference between these two loves, the common and saving:

> Beloved, we never should know Christ's love in all its heights and depths if He had not died; nor could we tell the Father's deep affection if He had not given His Son to die. As for the common mercies we enjoy, they all sing of 'love,' just as the sea-shell, when we put it to our ears, whispers of the deep sea whence it came; but ah! if you desire to hear the ocean itself, if you would hear the roarings of the floods, you must not look at every-day mercies, but at the mercies of that night, that day, that midday night, when Christ was crucified.[22]

WHOLE MEANING

Indeed, every individual has much to be grateful for. Whether they believe in Him or not, God's divine gifts of kindness are made available to behold and benefit from day-in, day-out. However, a frightful finish awaits the person who remains unaware of God's holiness.

---

22. Charles H. Spurgeon, *Spurgeon's Sermons: Volume 5* (Peabody: Hendrickson Publisher's Marketing, 2011). 335.

To be confronted with the whole truth about the love of God is to become aware of who God really is. Yet, many go about their days without any sort of God-awareness. Is this you? It will be evidenced by the decisions you make, the priorities you place—how you choose to live your life. Remember, we live out our view of God every single day. The knowledge of God is foundational to everything you and I do.

A GOD-AWARENESS

Semantics are of no help to us here—especially as it relates to a correct understanding about God the Creator and Redeemer. Unlike our usage of words and phrases—He is immutable (unchanging). God has no beginning and no end, therefore He is not subject to any such winds of change. He will always be the same. His attributes remain unaltered since the days of eternity past; and will do so throughout all eternity future. Thus, we must go to the Word of God to learn and interpret these attributes correctly. Only the Bible will give us an unfiltered view. What does it look like to have a God-awareness?

In the Old Testament, the prophet Isaiah writes of a vision he had received during the reign of a king named Uzziah.[23] Anointed at the young age of sixteen, Uzziah was

---

23. I am indebted to R.C. Sproul for any-and-everything gleaned from this passage (Isa. 6:1-8). He had preached on this text multiple times throughout his ministry (for example, 'Holy, Holy, Holy,' preached at the 2015 Ligonier National Conference, *After Darkness, Light* on Feb. 25, 2015. https://youtu. be/AgKzsZUmeBk); and he has written on the subject of God's holiness extensively. My favorite example being: *The Holiness of God* (Carol Stream: Tyndale House Publishers, 1985). Many of my words on these pages are his. No other man's ministry has helped to cultivate within me such a soul-gripping awareness of the holiness of God.

in power as king of Israel during the eighth century B.C., and it lasted for a full fifty-two years. Dr. Sproul observed that 'many people in Jerusalem lived their entire lives under the reign of King Uzziah.'[24] The kingdom was quite prosperous during Uzziah's rule. It even rivaled that of Solomon's, as the borders of the nation were expanded, the might of their military was strengthened, and an infrastructure was built like nothing ever seen before. These were good and glorious times.

THE PASSAGE'S METANARRATIVE

Chapter six begins with seven significant words that form the passage's metanarrative—the big picture or overarching storyline, 'In the year of King Uzziah's death' (Isa. 6:1a). This generation was unaccustomed to such loss. Their first would be their king, and when he had passed it became a time of national grief. It was an unbearable moment. There had been so few godly leaders in this nation's theocratic past (e.g., David and Hezekiah). The people loved and mourned this king—in much the same way America and a watching world did for President John F. Kennedy when he was gunned down in Dallas. Retired Secret Service Agent Clint Hill, the one seen jumping on the back of the presidential limousine on that tragic day of November 22, 1963, wrote in his book *Five Days in November*:

> Outside Parkland Hospital, the world has stopped. People listening to car radios pull over, unable to drive; women sob openly as men force back tears. Children struggle to understand why their parents, grandparents, and

---

24. Sproul, *The Holiness of God*, 23.

neighbors are crying. Whether they are young or old, black or white, the moment people hear the news is forever seared into their memories.[25]

Something similar had occurred on this day when Israel learned of their beloved king's death. God, through this man, had given them vision and hope. Much like royalty, Uzziah's reign had encouraged the people. But now he was gone; and the loss took its toll on them.

2 Chronicles 26 gives us some insight into how Uzziah died. As it turned out, the king did not finish well. Through his acquisition of great wealth and power this man tried to play God.[26]

Uzziah had pridefully sought a role that was not his. Kings were not to be priests, yet Uzziah entered the temple anyway. He did so against the wise counsel of eight priests (vv. 17-18). Uzziah was determined to burn incense in the sanctuary, regardless of the restrictions. He boldly did so, crossing the line of God's clear command. Sadly, the king's disobedience, a.k.a. his pride, resulted in a judgment of leprosy. Uzziah would live out his final days, 'in a separate house' (v. 21), discreetly in disgrace.

THE KING'S MAJESTY

What followed next was utterly ironic. During the death of this earthly king, Isaiah would receive a vision of *the* Definitive King! It would take his breath away. Sproul notes, 'The eyes of Isaiah were opened to see the real King of the

---

25. Clint Hill with Lisa McCubbin, *Five Days in November* (New York: Gallery Books, 2013), 116-19.

26. Sproul, *The Holiness of God*, 23.

nation.'[27] The prophet proclaimed, 'I saw the LORD sitting on a throne, lofty and exalted, with the train of His robe filling the temple' (Isa. 6:1). God is seen sitting on a throne in a posture of exaltation, and His robe (similar to that of the train of Princess Diana's wedding gown)[28] filled every square inch of the temple. In the ancient world, a king's magnificence, his importance, was often displayed by the size and beauty of his robe. And this one was a superb and supernatural train!

THE ANGELS' MAKE-UP

With the metanarrative of a grieving nation over the death of a beloved king now set, the anatomy of the angels is then described. Verse two, 'Seraphim stood above Him [God], each having six wings: with two he covered his face, and with two he covered his feet, and with two he flew.'

God creates His creatures for their habitats. Fish are designed to live in the water, and so they have scales and gills. Birds are made to roam in the air, and so they have feathers and wings. Polar bears are extraordinarily equipped for life in the Arctic—just look at their fur, skin, paws, and claws. These special angels seen by Isaiah are in the presence of God, and so they have two wings that cover their faces. This feature is vital to their survival. Synonymous to a solar eclipse, these seraphim cannot look directly at God's blinding light or it will cause permanent damage. His

---

27. Ibid, 26.

28. Lady Diana Spencer married Charles, the Prince of Wales, on July 29, 1981, at St. Paul's Cathedral in London. Her royal wedding dress' train was twenty-five feet long, included 10,000 pearls and sequins, and was seen by over 700 million people worldwide. http://news.bbc.co.uk/2/hi/uk_news/wales/6972870.stm

glory is so intense that even these angels must protect their eyes! Dr. Sproul adds:

> The seraphim are not sinful humans burdened with impure hearts. Yet as angelic beings, they are still creatures, and even in their lofty status as consorts of the heavenly host it is necessary for them to shield their eyes from a direct gaze on the face of God. They are fearfully and wonderfully made, equipped by their Creator with a special pair of wings to cover their faces in His majestic presence.[29]

That is just two of the angel's sets of wings. Another two wings are seen covering their feet. Why would this be necessary? Because they are mere creatures. Created beings. Do you recall the story of Moses and the burning bush? In Exodus 3:5 God warns, 'Do not come near here; remove your sandals from your feet, for the place on which you are standing is holy ground.' Why must he take off his sandals? What made this ground holy? It was the presence of a holy God! And to think, if that ground in Midian was called 'holy,' how much holier must heaven itself be!

The last two wings are mentioned as if it were a late addition—Isaiah describing that 'with two he flew.' These angels did with their wings what they had been created for: two for covering the eyes, two for the feet, and two to fly. Each set of appendages were designed with a specific purpose of being in the presence of God.

THE ANGELS' MESSAGE

However, all here is lost if we miss the angels' worshipful message of wonder. Isaiah describes for us from his vision

---

29. Sproul, *The Holiness of God*, 29.

a heavenly choir of two: 'And one called out to another and said, "Holy, Holy, Holy, is the LORD of hosts, the whole earth is full of His glory"' (6:3).

Often when we want to emphasize something today we use a literary device.[30] Sometimes *italics*, **bold print**, [brackets], exclamation points!!! or underlining will convey that what is being shared is of incredible importance. Another example of this is seen in the use of repetition. For example, Jesus would say 'truly, truly' to create this kind of emphasis. Literally, He was stating 'pay close attention to this truth!'[31] Yet, here we have something repeated not twice, but three times! It is not 'love, love, love' or even 'grace, grace, grace.' Instead, it is a triple declaration of the holiness of God.

WHAT WAS MOVED

Look what happens as their message, this offering of praise, is given by these angels. Something moves when a special message is given by them. 'And the foundations of the thresholds trembled at the voice of Him who called out' (6:4). What was moved? Everything and anything. Not only did the angels move, but the wood did, too. Every and any object was shaken to its core as a result of the holiness of God. Call it 'shock and awe.' They 'could neither hear nor speak but had the good sense to be moved by the presence of God.'[32]

---

30. Sproul, *The Holiness of God*, 30-31.

31. John 8:51 is a good example of such a use, 'Truly, truly, I say to you, if anyone keeps My word he will never see death.'

32. Sproul, *The Holiness of God*, 33

What's more, the prophet's vision moves Isaiah himself. He has seen God like never before. The One on the throne is not simply a God of love, but He is 'holy, holy, holy!' Isaiah's cry becomes one of mercy, 'Woe to me! For I am ruined! Because I am a man of unclean lips' (6:5).[33] He is cursing himself, and coming apart at the seams. He has a God-awareness. Sproul explains:

> The thing that quaked the most in the building was the body of Isaiah … He saw the holiness of God. For the first time in his life Isaiah really understood who God was. At the same instant, for the first time Isaiah really understood who Isaiah was … Isaiah was groveling on the floor. Every nerve fiber in his body was trembling. He was looking for a place to hide, praying that somehow the earth would cover him or the roof of the temple would fall upon him, anything to get him out from under the holy gaze of God. But there was nowhere to hide. He was naked and alone before God. He had no Eve to comfort him, no fig leaves to conceal him. His was pure moral anguish, the kind that rips out the heart of a man and tears his soul to pieces. Guilt, guilt, guilt. Relentless guilt screamed from his every pore.
>
> The holy God is also a God of grace. He refused to allow his servant to continue on his belly without comfort. He took immediate steps to cleanse the man and restore his soul. He commanded one of the seraphim to jump into action.[34]

---

33. The King James Version (KJV) reads, 'for I am undone!'

34. Sproul, *The Holiness of God*, 33, 37-38.

GOD'S MERCY

Isaiah in humility and repentance cried out to God for mercy. It was an unconditional surrender of his will, a cry of desperation, and in loving holiness God answered.[35] Isaiah continues, 'the seraphim flew to me with a burning coal in his hand, which he had taken from the altar with tongs. He touched my mouth with it and said, "Behold, this has touched your lips; and your iniquity is taken away and your sin is forgiven"' (6:6-7).

God in His loving holiness graciously opened this man's eyes. The 'son of Amoz' (1:1) known as Isaiah was persuaded of the glory of God. For he had a God-awareness that led to his own self-awareness. Isaiah received saving grace. The prophet was both forgiven and cleansed. This man of sin became a child of God. The one who claimed unclean lips had been promoted to prophet. The direction of his life changed because his understanding of God changed. Just as he was in awe of His God, so should we be.

The point here is that a God-awareness demonstrates the love of God.[36] This saving by a loving God rescues a person from the wrath of a holy God. Remember, just like Isaiah, we have sinned and fallen short of God's glorious standard.[37] And just like the seraphim, we are unable to gaze at Him.[38]

---

35. When a person cries out to God for mercy, He will answer. King David's dying words to his son Solomon affirms this, 'If you seek Him, He will let you find Him; but if you forsake Him, He will reject you forever' (1 Chron. 28:9).

36. 'But God demonstrates His own love toward us, in that while we were yet sinners, Christ died for us,' (Rom. 5:8).

37. 'for all have sinned and fall short of the glory of God,' (Rom. 3:23).

38. 'Who alone… dwells in unapproachable light,' (1 Tim. 6:16).

Heaven will not, and cannot be filled by those who reject God, refuse Christ, and remain in their sin.[39]

Standing before a small congregation in Enfield, Connecticut, on July 8, 1741, Jonathan Edwards addressed this very same subject. His sermon 'Sinners in the Hands of an Angry God' is one of the most famous messages ever to have been preached in America. Midway through his message Edwards stressed:

> The God that holds you over the pit of hell, much as one holds a spider, or some loathsome insect over the fire, abhors you, and is dreadfully provoked: His wrath towards you burns like fire; He looks upon you as worthy of nothing else, but to be cast into the fire; He is of purer eyes than to bear to have you in His sight; you are ten thousand times more abominable in His eyes, than the most hateful venomous serpent is in ours. You have offended Him infinitely more than ever a stubborn rebel did His prince; and yet it is nothing but His hand that holds you from falling into the fire every moment. It is to be ascribed to nothing else, that you did not go to hell the last night; that you were suffered to awake again in this world, after you closed your eyes to sleep. And there is no other reason to be given, why you have not dropped into hell since you arose in the morning, but that God's hand has held you up. There is no other reason to be given why you have not gone to hell, since you have sat here in the house of God, provoking His pure eyes by your sinful wicked manner of attending His solemn worship. Yea, there is nothing else

---

39. Universalism, the notion that everyone will be saved from the wrath of a holy God, and annihilationism, that those who are destined for heaven God takes to heaven and the rest He puts out of His existence, are two erroneous views. There is no biblical support for either.

that is to be given as a reason why you do not this very moment drop down into hell.[40]

Edwards' sermon was so powerfully received that the people began to cry out, 'What must I do to be saved?' It was as if the people and the pews shook from the very presence of God. At one point, 'there was such a breathing of distress, and weeping' that the preacher had to ask for silence in order that he might be heard by everyone in the church.[41] Again, their God-awareness of His loving holiness had led to a self-awareness of their own sin and need for a Savior.

Simply put, semantics will not suffice in summarizing the saving love of God. This kind of affection is reserved for those who repent and place their faith in Christ alone for forgiveness of their sins. He is love, yes. But He is also holy, holy, holy.

SUMMARY

- **The Half-Truth:** God is love. It is a phrase that has been sanitized and sentimentalized over time to insinuate that a loving God could never be a judging One, that the New Testament God is incompatible with the Old. After all, why shouldn't a person live as they desire to live—guilt- and shame-free?

- **The Whole-Truth:** God is love, *and He is holy, holy, holy*. Semantics has no sway on Scripture. The culture cannot change the biblical phrase's meaning or implied moral

40. Jonathan Edwards, *Sinners in the Hands of an Angry God* (Phillipsburg: P&R Publishing, 1992), 22-23.

41. Ibid, 4. This observation is made by John D. Currid in his foreword to the printed sermon by P&R Publishing.

standards. God's love as seen throughout the pages of Scripture is defined as both a common and saving grace. His *common grace* is a love that touches every man, woman, and child with *intellect* and *innovation*. God's *saving grace* is rooted in a *loving holiness* which resulted in the giving of His Son, Jesus Christ, to rescue and redeem us.

- **The Whole Meaning:** The prophet Isaiah's vision during an earthly king's reign provides us with an unfiltered view of the Definitive King. From the passage's *metanarrative*, *King's majesty*, and *angels' make-up*, to their *message*, *what was moved*, and *God's mercy*, Isaiah begins to understand His Creator and himself like never before. God is holy, holy, holy; and he is not. It is a moment of *God-awareness* that will ultimately lead to a *self-awareness*.

4.
HALF-TRUTH #4:
Jesus Is Truly a Man

Concerning Christ

It is 2 a.m. and you find yourself wide-awake. For whatever reason you are fully alert. Perhaps you heard a strange sound, or your bladder has been begging for the bathroom. Everyone else in the house is down for the count, including the dog. But you need to get up, which will involve *moving*. Moving from the collection of pillows, sheets, and blankets that have contributed to your comfort. Moving that will ensure an end to your beauty-sleep. This is a mandatory moving—a moving that must take place, but only after fifteen-minutes of internal conflict. 'It can wait. No, I really need to get up. Just a few more minutes. No, I have got to get up now!'

As soon as your feet hit the cold floor, the journey begins. 'Where are my slippers?' Either you are too exhausted or just plain lazy to search for them. And so, one bare foot follows after another. You're near a light switch—at least you believe you are, groping up-and-down the wall as if you have never been in this strange dark place before—when IT happens! Somehow, you have managed to step with all your weight on something plastic and pointed. The reality of this pain races from foot to mouth, like an erupting volcano. Without any kind of warning you exclaim—'#$@&%*!'

Hmmmm … what was it that you had shouted? No, really? What were those profane words? Something misdirected and fuel-injected? One way to make more of an injury or an affront is by adding what we call a 'swear' or 'curse' word. Proverbs 12:16 wisely records that with it 'a fool's anger is known at once.' Was it a swear word? More importantly, was it the Name of Jesus Christ?

The most shocking aspect of this is not in one's attempt to be obscene, but rather in its origin. You see, cursing comes straight from the heart. It is an inside job. If you want to know what is truly in your heart, listen for what comes out of your mouth when you unexpectedly step on something in the middle of the night—something like your child's LEGO minefield.[1]

I am both fascinated and flabbergasted by how many people will employ the Name of Jesus Christ as the exclamation point for their vexation. Countless uses—in the home, at the workplace, on the ballfield, throughout many of our superhero movies[2]—all testify to a society that

---

1. Jesus spoke to the Pharisees and scribes about this inward iniquity, 'The good man out of the good treasure of his heart brings forth what is good; and the evil man out of the evil treasure brings forth what is evil; for his mouth speaks from that which fills his heart' (Luke 6:45).

2. Ten instances in *Captain America: Civil War* alone. https://christiananswers.net/spotlight/movies/2016/captain america2016.html

does not see Him as a part of the eternal Godhead (i.e., the Trinity; which is the Father, the Son, and the Holy Spirit). There is no respect, no reverence, and no realization that the Name they use unreputably is the most reputable One of all. This Jesus will be their Judge.[3]

Today, most people would not dispute that Jesus lived fully as a man.[4] It is a notion they are willing to concede. A hill not worth dying on. But to declare that Jesus is God? They use His Name as if it were useless. They could not care less. This is why it is found in their index of invectives, sitting at the summit of their swear words, and employed as the epitome of all their expletives.

Dr. Philip Graham Ryken in his book, *Written in Stone: The Ten Commandments and Today's Moral Crisis*, tells the story of a Christian who had confronted two men on an airplane for breaking the Third Commandment—they were using God's Name in vain:

Some years ago, after a long speaking itinerary in the Midwest, I boarded a late-night flight to return home. I

---

3. In Philippians 2:9-11 we read that God the Father has 'highly exalted Him, and bestowed on Him the Name which is above every name, so that at the Name of Jesus every knee will bow, of those who are in heaven and on earth and under the earth, and that every tongue will confess that Jesus Christ is Lord, to the glory of God the Father.' Also, in the Gospel of John, 'For not even the Father judges anyone, but He has given all judgment to the Son' (5:22).

4. This was not always the case. Such a challenge occurred in the fifth century when Docetists (Hellenistic Greeks labeled from the word δοκέω, 'to appear') argued that Jesus only *appeared* to be human and to die. Their view was that He was completely divine, and therefore had no human nature. 'This is not a neat and tidy distinction, however. For example, Arianism—influenced by Greek philosophy—was also a denial of Christ's full humanity.' Michael Horton, *The Christian Faith: A Systematic Theology for Pilgrims on the Way* (Grand Rapids: Zondervan, 2011), 471.

was tired and looking forward to a rest. Sitting behind me in the airplane were two salesmen whose conversation was peppered with profanity. I had finally had it when they began running the Lord's Name into the gutter. I raised myself up from my seat and turned around so that I was looking down on them from my perch. Then I asked, 'Are either of you in the ministry?' The one in the aisle seat raised his eyebrows incredulously and said, 'What the… would ever make you think that?' 'Well, I am in the ministry.' I said with a smile. 'And I am amazed at your communication skills. You just said God, damn, hell, and Jesus Christ in one sentence. I can't get all of that into a whole sermon!' They both blushed, and I didn't hear another word from them for the remainder of the flight.[5]

Well-played! This man was creative with his confrontation. His aim was to get at the heart of their problem—or better yet, to pry open the eyes of their hearts. I believe it is safe to conclude that if those two salesmen had viewed Jesus Christ with any veneration whatsoever, then His Name would have been treated as sacred, not secular, holy, not common.

Gautama Buddha, Abu al-Qsim Muhammad, and Krishna-Vasudeva. While none of them are God, we all know they are never used as expletives, and for anyone to do so could result in an accusation of intolerance, or even an allegation

---

5. Philip Graham Ryken, *Written in Stone: The Ten Commandments and Today's Moral Crisis* (Phillipsburg: P&R Publishing, 2003), 95. The Third Commandment is found in Exodus 20:7 and reads, 'You shall not take the Name of the LORD your God in vain, for the LORD will not leave him unpunished who takes His Name in vain.'

of 'hate speech.'[6] Only the Name Jesus Christ is slandered in this way, none other.[7] In one outlandish outburst the Name of Jesus Christ is denigrated from that of a Holy Person to a haughty profanity, from the exalted Son of God to an exclaimed slur of man. To put it bluntly: Jesus Christ bore a curse for us, and became a curse word for others.

THE HALF-TRUTH

JESUS IS TRULY A MAN.

When a person takes the Name of Jesus in vain, they are, in effect, declaring a half-truth: that Jesus Christ is truly a man from history and nothing more—a mere mortal who was bound to a particular place, raised in the small Galilean village of Nazareth in the beginning of the first century.

It is accurate to say that Jesus lived truly as a man. The historical Jesus of Nazareth did exist. There is no legitimate scholar (Christian or non-Christian) who could knowledgeably deny His humanity. One of the most reliable extrabiblical accounts (i.e., outside of Scripture) comes from that of Publius Cornelius Tacitus. He was a first-century Roman senator and historian who viewed Christians as followers of 'the pernicious superstition' and cited in one of his writings that 'Christus, the founder of the name, was

---

6. 'Hate speech' is defined at Dictionary.com as 'speech that attacks, threatens, or insults a person or group on the basis of national origin, ethnicity, color, religion, gender, gender identity, sexual orientation, or disability.' http://www.dictionary.com/browse/hate-speech.

7. Continuing down this line of thought, in the Middle Ages 'certain vain oaths were believed to actually tear apart the ascended body of Christ, as He sat next to His Father in heaven.' http://newsfeed.time.com/2013/04/10/nine-things-you-probably-didnt-know-about-swear-words/

put to death by Pontius Pilate, procurator of Judea in the reign of Tiberius.'[8]

Other extraordinary extrabiblical examples from this time period include that of Gaius Suetonius Tranquillus, a secretary to the emperor of Rome (A.D. 117-138); Titus Flavius Josephus, a Jewish historian (A.D. 37-100); and Pliny the Younger, the Roman governor of Bithynia who wrote a letter to Emperor Trajan of Rome seeking advice on how to handle Christians (A.D. 111-112).[9]

Jesus was a living, breathing human being. It is a fact: He lived, and He died. Even those who spent time with Jesus never questioned His humanity. If you had heard, seen, and touched Him, would you?[10] I mean, face-to-face? Eye-to-eye? No. Of course not. The man Jesus from the town of Nazareth stood up to close inspection. He was real in every sense of the word. And as we'll explore later, He, in His humanity, lived much like any other human being. But that is still only half of the story. It is only half of the truth, intending to limit the One known as Jesus to the status of a safe and tame mortal.

Please keep reading—because the whole truth is about to catch you by the collar.

---

8. Written by Tacitus in A.D. 115, 'Annals' 15:44, in Henry Bettenson, ed., *Documents of the Christian Church* (New York: Oxford University Press 2nd ed., 1963), 1-2.

9. A treasure-trove of external sources like these can be found in F.F. Bruce's *Jesus and Christian Origins Outside the New Testament* (Grand Rapids: William B. Eerdmans Publishing Company, 1974).

10. 'What was from the beginning, what we have *heard*, what we have *seen* with our eyes, what we have looked at and *touched* with our hands, concerning the Word of Life,' (1 John 1:1, emphasis mine).

THE WHOLE-TRUTH

*JESUS IS TRULY A MAN **AND TRULY GOD.***

Regardless of how a person addresses Jesus Christ in this life, either with a swear or as their Savior, the reality of His dual nature remains. Jesus is man and God at the same time.[11] Two distinct natures, the human and the divine, in one whole Person. Not partly human and partly divine. Not humanly-divine or divinely-human. Not one to the exclusion of the other, and not even two people. It may sound simpler, yes, but it won't satisfy the claims of Scripture. Jesus is the Son of man and the Son of God. He is Jesus of Nazareth and Jesus the Christ. The Word of God is clear in this respect and to imply anything less is a half-truth.

In the Person of Jesus Christ both natures retained their own attributes. His humanity was always human and His deity always divine. He was born from His mother Mary as a baby, but has existed for all eternity as the Son of God the Father. Jesus lived, bled, and died, but He lives forevermore. Jesus went to the cross as our substitute, but He had never ever sinned.

Each of these statements deals with the duality of Jesus' natures: He is truly a man and truly God. They tell us that there is more to the story of this Jesus of Nazareth, much

---

11. Many will express this same truth with the words 'fully man, fully God.' However, there are those (myself included) who feel that the word 'fully' can sometimes confuse the issue. To say that Jesus was fully man—leaves no room for consideration of His divinity, because, well, He is full. As if you would be declaring that He is 100% human and nothing more because there is no room left in His Person. But Jesus was both fully human and fully divine. Two complete natures in one Person. How Chalcedon described it in A.D. 451 is preferable, '*vera homo, vera Deus*' or 'truly man and truly God.

more, because He claimed to be God and *is* God. Two realities, as the creature and the Creator. Two recognitions, as the sacrificial Lamb and the supreme Lord. Two roles, as a man and mankind's Mediator. The comparisons are endless! In order for us to understand better Jesus' bold assertions, let us look at His humanity and then His deity.

TRULY MAN

Opening your Bible is the first step to an unavoidable understanding of Who He really is. The New Testament is replete with references to Jesus' humanity. First, He was 'born of a woman' (Galatians 4:4). Jesus was born with a physical body from His mother, with a body like ours (you can read the account from Matthew 1:18-23 in its entirety below).[12] His journey in the birth canal was the same as ours. Jesus would humbly enter the world through a womb.[13]

---

12. Matthew 1:18-23, 'Now the birth of Jesus Christ was as follows: when His mother Mary had been betrothed to Joseph, before they came together she was found to be with child by the Holy Spirit. And Joseph her husband, being a righteous man and not wanting to disgrace her, planned to send her away secretly. But when he had considered this, behold, an angel of the Lord appeared to him in a dream, saying, "Joseph, son of David, do not be afraid to take Mary as your wife; for the Child who has been conceived in her is of the Holy Spirit. She will bear a Son; and you shall call His name Jesus, for He will save His people from their sins." Now all this took place to fulfill what was spoken by the Lord through the prophet: "Behold, the virgin shall be with Child and shall bear a Son, and they shall call His name Immanuel," which translated means, "God with us." And Joseph awoke from his sleep and did as the angel of the Lord commanded him, and took Mary as his wife, but kept her a virgin until she gave birth to a Son; and he called His Name Jesus.'

13. 'And she gave birth to her firstborn son' (Luke 2:7). This miraculous arrival of the Son of God through the virgin Mary is the beginning of Christ's earthly life and ministry. It is known as His incarnation, where the divine 'Word became flesh and dwelt among us' (John 1:14). The virgin birth was a mysterious work of the Holy Spirit within Mary's womb, making it possible for the Person Jesus to be truly a man.

Second, we also learn that Jesus lived as a child. Luke 2:41-52 contains the only reference (in all of the Gospel accounts) of Jesus in His youth. His parents had taken Him with them as they were traveling to Jerusalem for the Feast of the Passover, an annual feast to celebrate Israel's deliverance from Egypt by God (see Exodus 12:1-51). As they headed home to Nazareth, Jesus was lost and left behind. After much searching, Joseph and Mary would find their Son an astounding three days later. Can you imagine! But that's not the most interesting part. Where He was found was *teaching* the teachers of the law at the temple: 'And all who heard Him were amazed at His understanding and His answers' (v. 47).

Dr. Bruce Ware, professor of Christian theology at the Southern Baptist Theological Seminary, addresses this 'fascinating account of Jesus' as a twelve-year-old boy in his book *The Man Christ Jesus*. Ware writes:

> This remarkable account of Jesus' interaction with the teachers of the law in Jerusalem raises a very important question for our understanding of Jesus: just what accounts for the remarkable questions, answers, and understanding that Jesus evidenced in His conversations with these learned men? I think that many of us in the conservative evangelical tradition would have a ready answer. We would say, instinctively, the reason Jesus had such remarkable understanding of the law was that He was God in human flesh. After all, we might think, those Pharisees and teachers of the law didn't understand who they were dealing with. If they had only known the truth, that this twelve-year-old boy was none other than the incarnate God-man, they would have understood that His

wisdom came from His being God. So, given that He was God in human flesh, we reason, even as a twelve-year-old boy Jesus was able to astonish the greatest teachers in Israel.

I believe that this evangelical intuition, as we might call it, that Jesus' wisdom and understanding are accounted for by appeal to His deity, is not the answer that Luke, the Gospel writer, wishes us to see. Consider Luke 2:40 and 52, which function as bookends around this account of Jesus' childhood visit to Jerusalem. Luke 2:40 (ESV) records that 'the Child grew and became strong, filled with wisdom. And the favor of God was upon Him.' And Luke 2:52 (ESV) reads, 'And Jesus increased in wisdom and in stature and in favor with God and man.' Amazingly, what both of these verses indicate is that Jesus' wisdom is not a function of His divine nature but is the expression of His growth as a human being. One compelling reason for seeing this wisdom as His growing human wisdom is that Luke speaks of Jesus as growing in wisdom while also becoming stronger physically (increasing 'in wisdom and in stature'). So the wisdom that Jesus has, evidently, is a growing wisdom that parallels or accompanies His growth physically.[14]

Ware concludes that the twelve-year-old Jesus had an exemplary commitment to understand what the Scriptures taught, pointing out that 'As a boy, Jesus learned, no doubt, through the instruction of His parents, and from the teaching of the rabbis in His hometown of Nazareth, and

---

14. Bruce A. Ware, *The Man Christ Jesus: Theological Reflections on the Humanity of Christ* (Wheaton: Crossway, 2013), 48-49.

through His own diligent reading of God's Word. It was by these means that He grew and increased in wisdom.'[15]

Third, the Bible informs us that Jesus had all the trappings of a human body. He grew tired: 'So Jesus, being wearied from His journey, was sitting thus by the well' (John 4:6). He got thirsty, 'Jesus... said, "I am thirsty"' (John 19:28); and He grew hungry, 'And after He had fasted forty days and forty nights, He then became hungry' (Matthew 4:2). Turn to any one of the four Gospels and you can read of Jesus sharing many meals with many others.[16]

Fourth, as John Calvin puts it, 'Christ has put on our flesh, and also its feelings or affections.'[17] Throughout His earthly life, Jesus displayed a variety of emotions. He was surprised: 'Now when Jesus heard this, He marveled'[18] (Matt. 8:10). He was sorrowful: 'Then He said to them, "My soul is deeply grieved, to the point of death"' (Matt. 26:38). And He shed tears: 'He was deeply moved in spirit and was troubled, and said, "Where have you laid [Lazarus]?" They said to Him, "Lord, come and see." Jesus wept. So the Jews were saying, "See how He loved him!"' (John 11:33-36). Hebrews 5:7 adds, 'In the days of His flesh, He offered up both prayers and supplications with loud crying and tears.'

---

15. Ibid, 49.

16. Some examples found in the Gospel of Luke include: a banquet at Levi's home (5:27-32), at Simon's home (7:36-50), the feeding of the five thousand (9:10-17), on two occasions at a Pharisee's home (11:37-52; 14:1-24), and the Last Supper (22:14-38).

17. John Calvin, *Calvin Commentaries Volume XXII, 500th Anniversary Edition*, *Hebrews* (Grand Rapids: Baker Books, 2009), 108.

18. I like how the New International Version (NIV) uses the word 'amazed,' as in 'filled with wonder.'

Fifth, He expired. Not only did Jesus—truly as a man—experience birth, early childhood, and emotions, but there was a dreadful death with His humanity. When hanging on the cross, Jesus physically died. Scripture informs us that He had stopped breathing: 'And Jesus uttered a loud cry, and breathed His last' (Mark 15:37). Yes, His human heart had stopped beating and His human blood had stopped flowing. His living body was now lifeless. Again, from the Gospel of John, 'So the soldiers came … they saw that He was already dead,' (John 19:32-33).[19]

Every attribute, and every aspect of His humanity, was like ours with one exception: Jesus did not sin. His entire life was marked by sinlessness.[20] Take as an example, Matthew 21:12, where we read, 'Jesus entered the temple and drove out all those who were buying and selling in the temple, and overturned the tables of the money changers and the seats of those who were selling doves.' It was the second time He had done this (see John 2:13-16). Was He angry? Undeniably so! But it was a 'righteous anger,' not a fit of rage. It was never selfish nor was it ever sinful.

We are seldom marked by that kind of righteousness in our moments of rage. We are told to 'be angry, and yet do not sin' (Eph. 4:26). Yet most of our experiences with anger *are* selfish and sinful. Dr. David Powlison explains the contrasts between the two types in his book *Good & Angry*:

---

19. John MacArthur points out for us in his commentary on this passage, 'The soldiers were experts at determining death; it was a part of their job… Their testimony, and that of their commander (Mark 15:44-45), is irrefutable proof that Jesus was in fact dead.' *The MacArthur New Testament Commentary: John 12-21* (Chicago: Moody Publishers, 2008), 364.

20. 'He committed no sin, neither was deceit found in his mouth' (1 Pet. 2:22, ESV). Jesus lived as the perfect Man.

> Your anger is Godlike to the degree you treasure justice and fairness and are alert to betrayal and falsehood. Your anger is devil-like to the degree you play god and are petty, merciless, whiny, argumentative, willful, and unfair.[21]

As we considered this Jesus of Nazareth, the task of determining whether He was human or not was an easy one. An open-and-shut case. A shoo-in. His humanity has been firmly established. His existence is substantiated repeatedly by first century men both inside and outside of the New Testament.[22] But what about His deity? It is time for us to examine the second half of this whole truth: that Jesus Christ is truly God.

TRULY GOD

We all can understand how easy it is to acknowledge the Jesus of Nazareth; to accept the argument that is being made for His humanity. Standing on the side of His existence costs you and me nothing. To say Jesus existed as flesh and blood within the confines of space and time on planet earth is neither difficult nor demanding. 'Sure, I can agree to that,' someone might say. But what about His deity? Now that is an altogether different question.

This one puts everything at risk, including our words, our heart, even our actions! If you acknowledge that Jesus

---

21. David Powlison, *Good & Angry: Redeeming Anger, Irritation, Complaining, and Bitterness* (Greensboro: New Growth Press, 2016), 65-66.

22. I have only scratched the surface. For further evidence read Lee Strobel's *The Case for Christ*. Specifically chapter 4, 'The Corroborating Evidence' which answers the question: 'Is There Credible Evidence for Jesus Outside His Biographies?' (Grand Rapids: Zondervan, 1998), 73-91.

is 'the Christ, the Son of the living God' (Matt. 16:16), then your love and life must be shaped by His love and life.

Furthermore, it is not possible to consider Jesus as just a good man—or better yet, a good teacher. He was not claiming to be a good teacher. Underline this fact: Jesus Christ claimed to be God. You cannot get around this no matter how many attempts are made to attach accolades to His name. To declare Jesus as just another 'religious revolutionary,' or a person who was 'upright and upstanding,' misses the whole truth. Actually, it is a whole lie. He could not be only a spiritual mentor of any sort, because this is not what He had claimed to be. Jesus Christ claimed to be God, Lord of all, equal with God the Father in nature and essence.

There are only three choices that can be made when it comes to the deity of Jesus Christ. He is either a lunatic, a liar, or Lord. You will note that the category of Jesus being a 'good teacher' has been eliminated from this short list of possibilities. Unfortunately, it is no longer open as an option because of His claims to deity. We disregard the whole truth in saying that He was merely a good and moral man. Repeatedly, the Bible quotes Christ as saying otherwise. Look for yourself at just one profound example of such a claim; it is found in John 10:30-33, where Jesus explicitly told the Jewish authorities:

> 'I and the Father are one.' The Jews picked up stones again to stone Him. Jesus answered them, 'I showed you many good works from the Father; for which of them are you stoning Me?' The Jews answered Him, 'For a good work

we do not stone You, but for blasphemy; and because You, being a man, make Yourself out to be God.'[23]

Lunatic, liar, or Lord? We are left with nowhere else to go. That is it. These three options have been popularized as 'Lewis' Trilemma,' a label given to C.S. Lewis' argument for the deity of Christ found in his book *Mere Christianity*. Let's look at what he wrote:

I am trying here to prevent anyone saying the really foolish thing that people often say about Him: 'I'm ready to accept Jesus as a great moral teacher, but I don't accept his claim to be God.' That is the one thing we must not say. A man who was merely a man and said the sort of things Jesus said would not be a great moral teacher. He would either be a lunatic—on the level with the man who says he is a poached egg—or else he would be the Devil of Hell. You must make your choice. Either this man was, and is, the Son of God, or else a madman or something worse. You can shut him up for a fool, you can spit at him and kill him as a demon or you can fall at his feet and call him Lord and God. But let us not come with any patronising nonsense about his being a great human teacher. He has not left that open to us. He did not intend to... Now it seems to me obvious that He was neither a lunatic nor a fiend [devil]: and consequently, however strange or terrifying or unlikely it may seem, I have to accept the view that He

---

23. This is the fourth time that the Jews have tried to kill Jesus Christ in John's Gospel (see 5:16-18; 7:1; 8:59). Sadly, cults like the Jehovah's Witnesses and Mormons misinterpret this text to say that Jesus Christ was only expressing agreement with God the Father in regards to His agenda, not deity. The context strongly suggests that their interpretation is absurd.

was and is God. God has landed on this enemy-occupied world in human form.[24]

Lewis is spot on here. There are only three outcomes. For some will call Jesus Christ a *lunatic*, others will claim that He is a *liar*, and many will worship Him as *Lord*.

These same three options were available to those in Jesus' day, too. The text of Mark's Gospel, in chapter three, bears this out. Beginning with verse 21, Jesus' family members, 'His own people, were saying, "He has lost His senses."' In other words, they were calling Him a *lunatic*. They saw Him as a man who was literally out of His mind. Clearly, Jesus' own brothers had yet to believe in Him (see John 7:5). But this faulty view of their older half-brother would ultimately change, as they would declare Him to be Lord soon after His resurrection (see Acts 1:14; 1 Cor. 15:7).

---

24. C.S. Lewis, *Mere Christianity* (New York: Macmillan Publishing Company, 1960), 55-56. While this book is a Christian classic, an excellent evangelistic resource—I must for conscience's sake, note that I have always differed with Lewis substantially in some key areas of doctrine. So as to not detract from the above argument, you can find a number of these deficiencies detailed in Kevin DeYoung's blog post 'Cautions for Mere Christianity': https://www.thegospelcoalition.org/blogs/kevin-deyoung/cautions-for-mere-christianity/, as well as Southern Seminary's 'Elephant in the Room: Evangelicals Continue to Value C.S. Lewis Despite Theological Differences': http://equip.sbts.edu/publications/towers/elephant-in-the-room-evangelicals-continue-to-value-c-s-lewis-despite-theological-differences/. In the latter article, John Piper wisely warns that 'Lewis is not a writer to which we should turn for growth in a careful biblical understanding of Christian doctrine. There is almost no passage of Scripture on which I would turn to Lewis for exegetical illumination … His value is not in his biblical exegesis. Lewis is not the kind of writer who provides substance for a pastor's sermons.' Piper then adds that his value of Lewis' writings is found instead with 'the defense of truth.' I wholeheartedly concur.

In verse 22, Jesus' enemies, Israel's religious elite, 'the scribes … were saying, "He is possessed by Beelzebub"[25] and "He casts out demons by the ruler of demons."' The Pharisees and scribes were accusing the One who came from God to be a *liar*—claiming that He had actually come from the one who is called 'the father of lies' (John 8:44).

And in verse 29, a warning is made to those who would reject outright the witness of the Holy Spirit (the third Person of the Trinity), stating 'whoever blasphemes against the Holy Spirit.' This means the refusal to accept God's own testimony that Jesus Christ is *Lord*. How serious is this warning? Eternally serious. You may recall from the first chapter of this book that we had determined it was the Holy Spirit Himself who inspired the writing of the Bible— including the four Gospel accounts—which were 'written so that you may believe that Jesus is the Christ, the Son of God, and that by believing you may have life in His Name' (John 20:31).

The human nature of God was established by examining His birth, His childhood, a variety of His emotions, and His death upon the cross, as detailed in the pages of Scripture. It was easy to conclude that Jesus of Nazareth was truly a man.

---

25. 'Beelzebub' in the Old Testament referred to the 'Lord of the Flies,' a Philistine god that the Israelites called 'Baal-Zebul of Ekron' (see 2 Kings 1:2). John MacArthur writes in his commentary that 'By the first century, Beelzebul (or Beelzebub) had become the name for Satan, which is what the Pharisees intended when they associated that name with Jesus (cf. Matt. 10:25; Luke 11:15). Jesus' power could only be explained as coming from one of two sources: God or Satan… the leaders called Him a liar—whose power belonged instead to the prince of darkness.' *The MacArthur New Testament Commentary: Mark 1*-8 (Chicago: Moody Publishers, 2015), 181.

Equally so, the Bible is teeming with testimony of His divine nature. His perfections are revealed for us throughout the New Testament (especially in the Gospels), teaching us that Jesus Christ is indeed the Son of God. Undeniably, His attributes are one and the same with the Father's attributes. Let's look at just three instances before moving on to the whole meaning (of this whole truth) that Jesus is truly man and truly God.

First, Jesus is all-knowing, or 'omniscient.'[26] As God, He has 'direct cognition of everything in creation.'[27] If you have a Bible, turn to John 4. Here, Jesus is found sitting by a well around lunch time (v. 6, 'it was about the sixth hour'). He was 'wearied from His journey,' something that should no longer come as a surprise to us (the narrative begins by giving us a picture of His humanity). The sun is hot and high, and Jesus is tired and thirsty from a long journey. Then came a woman of Samaria to draw water from the well in the middle of the day instead of during the morning. She was likely an outcast, intentionally avoiding the early a.m. crowd. Even so, Jesus spoke with her. It was Jesus the Jew telling the Samaritan sinner all that she had already done. But how could He have known? The woman, who was visibly stunned by His omniscience, is later found in verse 29 compelling others to 'Come, see a Man who told me all the things that I have done; this is not the Christ, is it?' Yes, He is the Christ, the Son of God. Jesus knew it all. Nothing was hidden from His divine mind.

---

26. The prefix 'omni-' in each of these is from the Latin meaning 'all.'

27. Grenz, Guretzki, and Nordling, *Pocket Dictionary of Theological Terms,* 86.

Second, Jesus is all-present. Another word for this is omnipresent. He is everywhere as God. Even the name given to Him speaks of this attribute. 'Behold! The virgin will be with Child and will give birth to a Son, and they will call Him "Immanuel" (which means, "God with us")' (Matt. 1:23). Remarkably, the human birth of Christ would establish the divine presence of God with His people.

The promise of omnipresence is not only found here in the beginning of Matthew, but it is also seen in the middle and end of this Gospel.

The middle: Matthew quotes Jesus in 18:20, 'For where two or three have gathered together in My Name, I am there in their midst.' He is pledging (in the context of church discipline) to support and sustain faithful leaders as their God. These men can take solace in the fact that while they are confronting a person who is in sin, He is right there with them.[28]

The end: A refreshing reminder of His omnipresence is found in these final words to His body of believers in what is known as the Great Commission, 'and lo, I am with you always, even to the end of the age' (28:20). There is nothing in the entire created universe that lies outside the boundary of His care.[29] All things are present to Jesus because He is God. It is worth repeating: Jesus Christ is claiming to be God.

---

28. Grant Osborne in his commentary on this passage (vv. 15-20) adds, 'As they make their decision, certainly while in prayer, Jesus wants them to understand that He is with them ... Jesus is virtually declaring His divinity, for such a claim is possible only for God Himself.' *Exegetical Commentary on the New Testament: Matthew* (Grand Rapids: Zondervan, 2010), 688.

29. Grenz, Guretzki, and Nordling, *Pocket Dictionary of Theological Terms*, 86. They add under this definition for omnipresence, 'Perhaps [this term] more correctly suggests that all things are present to God.'

He has made a declaration of divinity to His disciples. He will never be absent or out-of-reach from us.

Finally, Jesus is all-powerful, or omnipotent. He is as strong as God, because He is God. There is no one like Him. No one is called 'almighty' in the Bible except for God. He is *El Shaddai*, a Hebrew name used frequently for God in the Old Testament meaning 'God Almighty.'[30] He is 'God Almighty' because His only restraint is a self-imposed one. And Jesus, as God, will only do what is consistent with His righteous character.

In Matthew 8, this is demonstrated by His power over the natural (vv. 23-27) and supernatural (vv. 28-34).

While on a boat with the disciples, 'there arose a great storm on the sea, so that the boat was being covered with waves… they came to Him… saying, "Save us, Lord; we are perishing!"' (vv. 24-25). Immediately after, the Son of God 'rebuked the winds and the sea, it became perfectly calm. The men were amazed, and said, "What kind of Man is this, that even the winds and the sea obey Him?"' (vv. 26-27). These men had witnessed firsthand the answer to their rhetorical question. As the text stated, they were amazed, astounded, and in awe. Why? He is omnipotent—Lord over all that is natural.

Next we move from mortal men to fallen angels, from being amazed to being alarmed. This passage tells us that a mass of demons had possessed two men.[31] When con-

---

30. An example of this is found in Exodus 15:6, 'Your right hand, O Lord [*El Shaddai*], is majestic in power, Your right hand, O Lord [*El Shaddai*], shatters the enemy.'

31. Mark 5:9 actually gives us their name (or title) which is 'Legion.' This was a Roman military designation representing up to six thousand soldiers.

fronted by Jesus 'they cried out, saying "What business do we have with each other, Son of God? [Note: they recognize Jesus as God!] Have You come to torment us before the time?"... The demons began to entreat Him, saying "If You are going to cast us out, send us into the herd of swine"' (vv. 29, 31). Don't miss this: the Son of God uttered only one word, 'Go!' (v. 32).[32] They had no choice but to submit and surrender. Why? He is omnipotent; Lord over all that is supernatural.[33]

Again, we only examined (albeit briefly) three of the attributes of God: His omniscience, omnipresence, and omnipotence. But there are more. Many more. For every attribute God has, Jesus has. Everything essential to being God, Jesus possesses. Jesus Christ is truly God.

WHOLE MEANING

We understand Jesus to be one Person with two natures—a human nature which was evidenced by how He lived and died, and a divine nature which was exemplified by the use of His attributes while on this earth. Jesus Christ is truly man and truly God. This is critically important for us, if we are not only to understand the Person of Christ, but His work on the cross.

Therefore, the response of these demons to Jesus, 'for we are many,' is an accurate one!

32. Mark 5:13 aptly reads, 'Jesus gave them permission.' Jesus permitted them passage; He ratified their relocation. All because of His omnipotence. The following phrase is helpful and has long been attributed to Martin Luther, 'Satan is on a leash, whose length is determined by God.'

33. The demons' theology (the study of God) is correct; they know the truth about Jesus. James also makes this clear in his epistle, 'You believe that God is one. You do well; the demons also believe, and shudder' (2:19).

You see, Jesus had to be human in order to become the perfect substitute for humanity. Otherwise, He could not be the Savior of humans. Hebrews 2:14 is helpful here: 'Therefore, since the children share in flesh and blood, He Himself likewise also partook of the same, that through death He might render powerless him who had the power of death, that is, the devil.' He had to take our nature upon Himself in order to be our substitute. Because we are human, Jesus became human. And by becoming human, He could die.[34]

In Old Testament times, God had instructed His people, the Israelites, to perform animal sacrifices. They were required to do so regularly, and with specific instructions on the kind of animal and the procedures involved. However, these sacrifices did not pay for their sins against God. Hebrews 10:4 makes this clear in that, 'it is impossible for the blood of bulls and goats to take away sins.' Then why would God have required them? How could God receive this kind of payment and forgive the Old Testament believers of their sins when He clearly states that it would not clear them of their debt?

Dr. Ware is once again instructive to us. He writes in his book *The Man Christ Jesus*:

> The answer is astonishing, and brings us to Jesus, the one-and-only sacrifice that actually could atone for our sin. The efficacy [effectiveness] of those Old Testament animal sacrifices rested not in themselves but altogether in what they pointed to. They were 'types' of the greater

---

34. A marvelous nine minute video exposition of this passage by John Piper can be found here: https://www.desiringgod.org/labs/why-christmas

sacrifice that was to come. They pointed to the planned and purposed and certain coming of 'the Lamb of God' (John 1:29), whom the Father would offer for the people, the divine-human Lamb who could actually remove the sin of all those who believed the promises of God.[35]

To think, the sacrifices of old were pointed—connected to the divine plan of God the Father. He wholly offered His Son as the 'one-and-only sacrifice that could actually atone for sin.' Ware continues with this analogy:

[C]onsider what happens when you buy something with a credit card. Suppose you're in the mall, and you find some shoes you like. You can take those shoes up to the register, charge them to your credit card, and walk out of that store with your new shoes, having paid absolutely nothing for them! Why is this not shoplifting? Why are you not stopped at the door by the security guard and charged with stealing? You are free to leave with the shoes because you have entered into a legal transaction whereby you have obligated yourself to a future payment by which you (and others) may now consider those shoes as your own. Even though you have not paid a penny for them, you have tied yourself legally to an agreement (that's what you've done, by the way, when you sign the credit card slip) by which those shoes will be paid for by you at some agreed-upon date in the future. So, while the shoes are legally yours, they are only paid for when the credit card statement comes and a payment is made from your bank account.

In a similar way, God forgave the sin of all Old Testament saints; as if it were, on credit. He devised a system of

---

35. Bruce A. Ware, *The Man Christ Jesus,* 119-20.

> sacrifices by which each of those animal sacrifices would signal His obligation, at some point in the future, to ensure that the payment for those sins would surely and truly be made… Apart from that future payment, those animal sacrifices were totally useless.[36]

Why is it of such great importance to us today to understand the Person and work of Christ? Because God provided a sinless human sacrifice. It was Jesus who shared our 'flesh and blood' (Heb. 2:14), and He did so truly as the perfect Man. Ware concludes, 'The credit card statement has come, the check is written, and the payment accepted! This is what God has done in the offering of His Son, who alone could make the payment in full for our sin.'[37]

But that is only half of the whole meaning. We must remember that Jesus is truly a man and *truly God*. His divine nature is also necessary if He is to be our Mediator. A mediator is 'a person who attempts to make people involved in a conflict come to an agreement; a go-between.'[38] And the conflict we (mankind) have with God remains irreconcilable without the efforts of this Mediator.

How did this happen? Man has separated himself from God by his own sin.[39] This originally occurred in the Garden

---

36. Ibid, 121-22.

37. Ibid, 123.

38. *English Oxford Living Dictionary.* https://en.oxforddictionaries.com/definition/mediator

39. Isaiah 59:2 says, 'But your iniquities have made a separation between you and your God, and your sins have hidden His face from you so that He does not hear.'

of Eden with Adam and Eve,[40] and is now repeated by every man, woman, and child, multiple times every single day. We don't need to teach a child how to sin. They come fully-equipped with this feature—as do we all.

What is sin? Sin is the breaking of God's Law. (We break our own laws, not to mention God's.) And the penalty for doing so, for violating His commands, is death.[41] News flash: our death is not the result of natural causes—it is God's curse on humanity due to our rebellion against Him and His will. This curse, man's punishment, is both physical and eternal.[42]

Who can come between God and mankind to resolve this conflict? To reconcile sinners? Only Jesus. 'For there is one God, and one Mediator also between God and men, the man Christ Jesus,' (1 Tim. 2:5). Jesus Christ is truly a man, and truly God. He is the only One who could fulfill this role.

---

40. Genesis 3:6 says, 'When the woman saw that the tree was good for food, and that it was a delight to the eyes, and that the tree was desirable to make one wise, she took from its fruit and ate; and she gave also to her husband with her, and he ate.'

41. Romans 6:23, 'For the wages of sin is death, but the free gift of God is eternal life in Christ Jesus our Lord.'

42. Revelation 20:11-15 says, 'Then I saw a great white throne and Him who sat upon it, from whose presence earth and heaven fled away, and no place was found for them. And I saw the dead, the great and the small, standing before the throne, and books were opened; and another book was opened, which is the book of life; and the dead were judged from the things which were written in the books, according to their deeds. And the sea gave up the dead which were in it, and death and Hades gave up the dead which were in them; and they were judged, every one of them according to their deeds. Then death and Hades were thrown into the lake of fire. This is the second death, the lake of fire. And if anyone's name was not found written in the book of life, he was thrown into the lake of fire.'

Only a truly human nature could represent us to God; and only a truly divine nature could represent God to man.[43]

Where did this reconciliation take place? On the cross of Calvary one Person with two natures enacted a great exchange—known as the great doctrine of substitution. Here is what made it so great: 'He made Him who knew no sin to be sin on our behalf, so that we might become the righteousness of God in Him' (2 Cor. 5:21). Jesus Christ, as truly man and truly God, became the only possible sacrifice for our sin. He became our sinless substitute.

John MacArthur powerfully unpacked this verse for Kirk Cameron during a television interview in 2009:

> [John MacArthur] It is the greatest gospel verse in the Bible ... let me unpack those fifteen Greek words.
>
> 'He,' God, 'made Jesus sin.' What do you mean 'He made Jesus sin'? Only in one sense, He treated Him as if He had committed every sin ever committed by every person who would ever believe though in fact He committed none of them.
>
> Hanging on the cross He was holy, harmless, and undefiled. Hanging on the cross He was a spotless Lamb. He was never for a split-second a sinner. He is holy God on the cross. But God is treating Him, I'll put it more practically, as if He lived *my life*.
>
> God punished Jesus for my sin; turns right around and treats me as if I lived His life.
>
> That's the great doctrine of substitution; and on that doctrine turned the whole reformation of the Church. That is the heart of the gospel. And what you get is

---

43. Wayne Grudem, *Systematic Theology: An Introduction to Biblical Doctrine* (Leicester: Inter-Varsity Press: 2000), 541.

complete forgiveness, covered by the righteousness of
Jesus Christ—when He looks at the cross He sees you, and
when He looks at you He sees Christ.

[Kirk Cameron] If there is one thing in my life I want to
make sure I understand, that's it. It is the gospel.[44]

Everything we believe depends on this. May we marvel
at the Person and work of Jesus Christ by confessing with
Thomas that He is 'My Lord and my God!' (John 20:28). Let
us cry out along with Peter, 'You are the Christ, the Son of
the living God' (Matt. 16:16). Both of these disciples had it
right: Jesus is truly a man, and truly God.

SUMMARY

- **The Half-Truth:** Jesus is truly a man. Most would not
  dispute that the historical Jesus of Nazareth existed.
  No legitimate scholar would deny it; and those who
  spent time with Jesus never questioned it. However,
  when a person takes the Name of Jesus in vain, they
  are, in effect, declaring that He is a man from history
  and nothing more. It is an attempt to make the Holy
  Person a haughty profanity, the exalted Son of God an
  exclaimed slur of man.

- **The Whole-Truth:** Jesus is truly a man *and truly God*.
  His humanity was like ours (with one exception: Jesus
  did not sin); and His divine attributes are one and the
  same with the Father's (e.g., omniscience, omnipresence, and omnipotence). Regardless of how a person
  addresses Jesus Christ in this life, either with a swear

---

44. Well worth one-and-a-half minutes of your viewing time: https://youtube/
SZuVt7qWO80

or as their Savior, the reality of His dual nature remains. You cannot cop-out with a claim that He was a 'good teacher.' He is either a lunatic, liar, or Lord.

- **The Whole Meaning:** Jesus had to be a human in order to be the perfect substitute for humanity. Otherwise, He could not be the Savior of humans. His divine nature was also necessary to be our Mediator. Only a truly human nature could represent us to God; and only a truly divine nature could represent God to man. On the cross of Calvary one Person with two natures enacted a great exchange. Jesus Christ, as truly man and truly God, became the only possible sacrifice for sin, as our sinless substitute.

5.
HALF-TRUTH #5:
Our Good Deeds Matter

Concerning Faith

Grading on a curve is widely used in universities today. Ask a parent for an opinion on institutions encouraging professors to inflate students' grades, and you will find many appalled to learn the practice actually exists and is publicly endorsed. (At least we hope they are appalled.) Why? Because grading on a curve will ultimately hurt—not help—young adults by assigning grades comparatively instead of objectively to them. Common sense dictates that classrooms set kids up to fail when a student's assessment is far from authentic, and the standard they are being prepared for is nowhere near what it seems. The bar becomes a bell curve. The level gets lowered, and the scale slides.

But it is an uncomfortable reality in many of our schools. As one UCLA law prof put it, 'The pressures for grade inflation are quite real, and flow from basic human nature: Most teachers don't like giving students low grades, especially once they've gotten to know their students relatively well.[1] This sounds like another epidemic of ours, where every child who participates in a sports activity receives a trophy regardless of whether they win, lose, or draw—basically a 'no losers' zone.

Both are the result of a new self-esteem trend where everything is to be viewed like a Happy Meal with a prize inside.

Wasn't the biggest problem inside the classroom with students cheating, and not the teachers? I can remember my high school history teacher handing out his exams with a stern warning to 'keep your eyes on your own papers!' Admittedly, I was one of those culprits. A few of us had a pretty good system in place to determine the answer to an unknown question. Suffice it to say, our signals fell somewhere between the Morse code and a Vulcan mind-meld. I can only imagine the avenues available to a student today via Google and a mobile device.

And yet again, here is what a teacher from a prominent law school wrote in a column for *The New York Times*:

> Ask people what's wrong in American higher education, and you'll hear about grade inflation. At Harvard a few years ago, a professor complained that the most common grade was an A-. He was quickly corrected: The most common grade at Harvard was an A. Across 200 colleges and universities, over 40 percent of grades were in the

---

1. Eugene Volokh, 'In Praise of Grading on a Curve,' *The Washington Post* (February 9, 2015), accessible online at: https://www.washingtonpost.com/news/volokh-conspiracy/wp/2015/02/09/in-praise-of-grading-on-a-curve/

A realm. At both four-year and two-year schools, more students receive A's than any other grade—a percentage that has grown over the past three decades.[2]

When scouring the Internet, a number of related articles and blog posts all seemed to cite this same study, whereby an astounding seventy years of grading in America's colleges and universities was collected and analyzed. The paper, published by Teachers College of Columbia University, looked at 200 four-year colleges and universities with a total enrollment of some 1.5 million students. The report says, excellence is becoming obsolete. 'As a result of instructors gradually lowering their standards, A has become the most common grade on American college campuses. Without regulation, or at least strong grading guidelines, grades at American institutions of higher learning likely will continue to have less and less meaning.'[3]

People tend to view their entrance into eternity the same way, as if God is grading on a curve. Look, He's a nice guy, and He is concerned that you feel positive about your efforts. He wants you to know He sees them, and has devised a process where He will take all of humanity's test

2. Adam Grant, 'Why We Should Stop Grading Students on a Curve,' *The New York Times* (September 10, 2016), accessible online at: https://www.nytimes.com/2016/09/11/opinion/sunday/why-we-should-stop-grading-students-on-a-curve.html. Grant is also concerned about another practice by professors, 'the opposite problem worries me even more: grade *deflation*. It happens whenever teachers use a forced grading curve: The top 10 percent of students receive A's, the next 30 percent get B's, and so on. Sometimes it's mandated by institutions; sometimes it's chosen by teachers.'

3. Stuart Rojstaczer and Christopher Healy, 'Where A Is Ordinary: The Evolution of American College and University Grading, 1940–2009,' *Teachers College Record*, Vol. 114, No. 7 (Teachers College of Columbia University, 2012), 4. Available online at: http://www.tcrecord.org/Content.asp?ContentId=16473.

scores, find an average, and adjust the grades. As long as you are living (relatively speaking) better than someone else, you will most likely pass 'go,' collect $200, and enter into a place of blessing. When you participate in some good deeds, you'll be guaranteed a trophy. You can feel satisfied in yourself and your own abilities because being 'a good person' will merit you an A in heaven.

Still unsure of your eternal destiny? Not to worry. You can feel even better about your 'chances' by performing any number of these good works. Here are a few deeds considered to be worth a great deal of points to God in His grading:

- Can you count the ways you have cared for children? (Not bad, as this is helpful.)

- Did you ever donate to a disease drive? (Now that was good.)

- Have you ever helped the hungry or homeless? (Even better.)

- Were you ever willing to work for someone else's welfare? (One of the best.)

Sarcasm aside, this is not to say we should be indifferent to the suffering that surrounds us. Nor are we to run from opportunities which compel us to be compassionate. Most certainly, we are to be a generous people who care enough to give of our time and money to help others in need. Good deeds, in this sense, *are* good. However, if your understanding is that these acts assist in any way to secure a right standing before a holy and just God, you will be sorely mistaken on that day—a day when all will stand before Him in final judgment. A day when you will make an attempt to explain how your good deeds are sufficient to save yourself.[4]

THE HALF-TRUTH

OUR GOOD DEEDS MATTER.

The half-truth in this chapter has much in common with the professors who are inflating their students' grades. Those kids will be led to believe they have passed the class, only to learn later how unprepared they really are for the real world. Similarly, there is a belief that people will get to heaven as a result of God grading on a scale. Some would express this view by insisting, 'As long as my life is less sinful than the next person, I should be good enough to make it into heaven.'

Frankly, it is naive to think a person's good works could ever cause the balance to tilt in their righteous favor. Call it a miscalculation at best. It is a pretense to point to a man's score on a curve, instead of Christ's sacrifice on the cross. Our good deeds will never merit our own salvation. To merit it would mean that we could actually do something on our own to earn it, which we can't. Or even deserve it, which we don't. And yet, this is exactly what is advertised abroad. Every man-made religion is marketing that our good deeds matter to enter eternity—some lead with it, while others

---

4. Jesus' words, as recorded in Matthew 7:21-23, are some of the most terrifying truths a person might ever hear from Him: 'Not everyone who says to Me, "Lord, Lord," will enter the kingdom of heaven, but he who does the will of My Father who is in heaven will enter. Many will say to Me on that day, "Lord, Lord, did we not prophesy in Your Name, and in Your Name cast out demons, and in Your Name perform many miracles?" And then I will declare to them, "I never knew you; depart from Me, you who practice lawlessness."' He is essentially telling those who have trusted in their good deeds for entrance into heaven to 'go to hell.'

mislead around it. Survey them and you will find works to be their common denominator.

Take, as an example, Islam's god Allah, whose followers believe he will evaluate people on a scale of absolute justice, weighing one's good deeds against one's bad deeds. This final judgment is established entirely upon the testimony of two recording angels, who have been assigned to each person to keep track of their life's activities. For the Muslim, the hope of paradise rests on how their works will fair upon Allah's scale.[5] Quoting from the Quran, 'Those whose balance [of good deeds] is heavy—they will attain salvation; but those whose balance is light, will be those who have lost their souls; and in hell will they abide' (Surah 23:102-103).

Another example is found within the belief system of Jehovah's Witnesses. Good deeds are absolutely necessary if a Witness is to be made eligible for eternal life. Their own publication proclaims, 'To get one's name written in that Book of Life will depend upon one's works ... [they are to be] working hard for the reward of eternal life.'[6] This hard work includes membership into the Watchtower Society, an organization they believe to be the sole arbiter of God on earth. They add, 'If we are to walk in the light of truth we must recognize not only Jehovah God as our father but his organization as our 'mother.'[7]

---

5. For more information, see Ron Rhodes' quick reference guide, *Islam: What You Need to Know* (Eugene: Harvest House Publishers, 2000). He has created these helpful 'What You Need to Know' pamphlets on a variety of subjects.

6. Quoted in *The Watchtower*, April 1, 1947, 107. All issues are accessible online at http://avoidjw.org/magazines/.

7. This is also taken from their publication *The Watchtower*, May 1, 1957, 274. A later edition echoes the errant belief, 'To receive everlasting life in the

There are many more religions we could survey—all boiling down to a works-based theology in order to gain some kind of access to an afterlife. Have you heard about Buddhism's Noble Eightfold Path? Or Christian Science's reflection of the divine mind? Perhaps Hinduism's practice of yoga? Judaism's keeping of the Law and its ceremonies? Mormonism's fulfilment of ordinances? Roman Catholicism's list of required sacraments?

We should not be surprised at the number of ways man has devised to save himself. Yet, as we will soon see, they all lead to his eternal destruction. In fact, that is exactly what Jesus had warned the multitudes in Matthew 7:13 when He said that, 'the gate is wide and the way is broad that leads to destruction, and there are many who enter through it.'

WHOLE TRUTH

OUR GOOD DEEDS MATTER, **WHEN PRECEDED BY FAITH**.

Before moving any further down the page we must set the record straight: salvation is not based on our own goodness, but rather on the goodness of Jesus Christ. There can be no works added to what Christ has already done on the cross. Your decency and kindness will grant no favor with God. It is Jesus + nothing, not Jesus + decency, not Jesus + kindness, not even Jesus + something religious. God grades on the *cross* not on the *curve*.[8]

---

earthly Paradise we must identify that organization and serve God as a part of it,' February 15, 1983, 12.

8. This phrase is not original with me and has often been attributed to the late Dr. Adrian Rogers, *ADRIANISMS: The Collected Wit and Wisdom of Adrian Rogers* (Collierville: Innovo Publishing, 2015), 14.

Ultimately, there is only one question to be found on God's final exam: 'Who do you say I [Jesus] am?'[9] To flat-out deny Jesus Christ as the Son of God, who came in the flesh to take away our sins, is to not only fail the test but to forego taking it. Again, there is only one question on this paper. Many have refused to take a look at it; and for that act of superiority, they will receive an automatic zero. A failing grade. There is nothing else you or I can do to affect the outcome of our score. No good works, or even religious works for that matter, will save us.

The reality is that the best behavior of an unbeliever is seen in God's eyes as nothing more than a 'filthy garment.' These two significant words are found in Isaiah 64:6 where we read, 'For all of us have become like one who is unclean, and all our righteous deeds are like *a filthy garment.*' Our works before God are impure because our own sin has stained it. Sin ruins everything it touches within a human— emotions, intellect, and will. Our attitudes become self-arrogant, our purposes self-promoting, and our desires self-deceiving. The prophet Isaiah graphically illustrates this by referring to a used menstrual cloth during a woman's period. This is his point: God sees the best deeds of man as utterly unclean. They have been sullied by sin.

The 'filthy garment' is in direct contrast to the 'salvation and righteousness that believers will wear' when receiving Jesus' work on the cross by faith.[10] God promises a passing

---

9. These words were asked of Peter by Jesus Christ in Matthew 16:15. He answered, 'You are the Christ [the promised Messiah of the Old Testament], the Son of the living God' (v. 16).

10. Gary V. Smith, *New American Commentary: Isaiah 50-66, vol. 15b* (Nashville: B&H Publishing Group: 2009), 691.

grade when we answer the question correctly, when we respond in faith to the finished work of Christ on the cross. He also promises to cleanse our impurity, for we read, 'Though your sins are as scarlet, they will be as white as snow; though they are red like crimson, they will be like wool' (Isa. 1:18). There's even a trophy![11]

Take notice there are only two types of works we have been discussing in this chapter: the works of man and the work of Christ. Dr. Steve Lawson explains in his book *Heaven Help Us*:

> All the religions of the world can be put into one of two categories. On one side, there's the religion of human achievement. On the other side, there's the religion of divine accomplishment. All religions, except one, teach that man must do good works and earn His way to Heaven. Only Christianity teaches that salvation is a free gift offered to undeserving sinners on the basis of the finished work of Christ at the cross. Only faith in Christ saves.
>
> That's why in Heaven we will be praising Christ. We will not be praising ourselves, because no amount of good works, church membership, baptismal certificates, or service can take away sin. Only Christ can save us from sin.[12]

Therefore, your answer on God's final exam will be predicated upon what you believe merits (or earns) a passing grade. Is it

---

11. James 1:12, 'when he passes the test he will receive the crown of life that God has promised to those who love Him' (HCSB). The 'crown of life' can literally be translated from the original Greek as 'the crown that is life.' A promise has been made to those who love God—and it is eternal, everlasting life with Him in heaven.

12. Steven J. Lawson, *Heaven Help Us! Truths About Eternity That Will Help* (Colorado Springs: NavPress, 1995), 92.

man-centered or Christ-centered? Works-centered or Christ's work-centered? Something you can earn or something Christ has given? Will it be the curve or the cross?

MAN'S WORKS

The grade given for man's works is always a failing one, because they have absolutely nothing to do with Christ's work on the cross. Every single effort to save ourselves in our own strength is worthless—every single time.[13] It is an empty work when it is a Christ-less work, a work that rests on the merits of man and not on Christ. We fail, fall, and fumble in our labor to be holy without the help of the Holy One. We are incapable of earning His favor on our own.

Perhaps you are thinking, 'Why is this such an issue? Hasn't he heard that if everyone did something good every single day, the world would be a much better place?' Sending good thoughts out into the universe is not only Buddhist, it is temporal. Yes, I am all for treating one another with honor, but that will not change our sinful status before a holy God. Please get this: you and I are unable to do one single sinless work in our own strength. Seriously. Forget the notion that your good works will outweigh your bad ones. This is a baseless belief. You don't even have a good work. No, not one!

'Not true,' you declare. Okay, then give me your best work. Put the book down for a moment to see if you can conjure up an action of yours for an honest evaluation. But not simply a good work—pick something stellar, one of your very best moments. A brag-worthy story. Don't worry, I'll wait…

---

13. Paul writes in Romans 14:23 that 'whatever is not from faith is sin.'

Got it? Great, let's evaluate this deed from the proper perspective—God's.

It is imperative that we begin with His definition of sin, which is 'lawlessness,' or the rejection of the law of God. We learn in 1 John 3:4 that, 'Everyone who practices sin also practices lawlessness; and sin is lawlessness.' Paul expands on this for us in Romans 8:7 when he says, 'the mind set on the flesh is hostile toward God; for it does not subject itself to the law of God, for it is not even able to do so.' A diagnosis is being made here that man, specifically in his mind and will, is infected with a disposition towards lawlessness. He refuses to yield because of sin. It is 'a nature that is oriented away from God.'[14] Man is unable (in his flesh) to submit completely to what God desires and requires of him.

John Piper, the founder-teacher of *Desiring God* ministries, describes this inherent sin as 'any feeling or thought or speech or action that comes from a heart that does not treasure God over all other things.'[15] It is a love of anything or anyone above God. Its aim is to elevate self. To be more precise, we can pinpoint this as the deadly sin of pride.[16] Jonathan Edwards labeled pride as 'the most hidden, secret, and deceitful of all sins.'[17] While the prideful philosophy of humanism believes man is basically good—with no form

---

14. Lambert, *A Theology of Biblical Counseling*, 217.

15. Taken from John Piper's message 'What Is Sin? The Essence and Root of All Sinning,' given at the Desiring God 2015 Conference for Pastors in Bethlehem, MN. Accessible at: https://www.desiringgod.org/messages/the-origin-essence-and-definition-of-sin.

16. Psalm 10:4 says, 'In his pride the wicked man does not seek Him; in all his thoughts there is no room for God' (NIV).

17. From Jonathan Edwards, *Advice to Young Converts*, as quoted in C.J. Mahaney's *Humility: True Greatness* (Sisters: Multnomah, 2005), 30.

of moral evil ever penetrating the core—the Bible sets us straight, teaching us that this smug face of self-exaltation[18] has permeated every aspect of our lives. (This is where your best work comes in.) Piper continues on the subject of sin:

> Sin is our preference for anything over God. Sin is our disapproval of God. Sin is our exchange of His glory for substitutes. Sin is our suppression of the truth of God. Sin is our heart's hostility to God. It is who we are to the bottom of our hearts. Until Christ.
>
> So can such sinners do good works—build hospitals, keep the speed limit, negotiate peace, heal diseases, feed the poor, pay a fair wage? And of course the answer from one angle is yes… [but] there is another angle from which to look. A biblical angle.
>
> The other angle starts in Romans 3:10, 12, (ESV) 'None is righteous, no, not one; … no one does good, not even one.' From this angle, without Christ we cannot do good. The writer to the Hebrews puts it like this: 'Without faith it is impossible to please God' (Heb. 11:6). And Paul puts it like this: 'Whatever does not proceed from faith is sin' (Rom. 14:23 ESV).
>
> In other words, the reason some deeds of unbelievers are called 'good' in the New Testament is because in the ordinary use of language we sometimes describe deeds according to ordinary human standards. Committing adultery is bad. Not committing adultery is good.
>
> But there is another angle. If not committing adultery comes from a heart that has no love for God and treasures

---

18. I love this phrase (and chapter) Jason Meyer has written in the little book *Killjoys: The Seven Deadly Sins*, Marshall Segal editor (Minneapolis: Desiring God, 2015), 10. He also calls pride 'a cosmic crime,' and that 'As finite creatures, we cannot fully grasp God's infinite revulsion against pride's rebellion. God hates pride,' 9.

many things more than God, then that act of chastity is not an expression of love to God. It's not a way of expressing His value. And so it is a dishonor to God. He is neglected, ignored, not a decisive factor, and in that sense the fruit of that heart is not good ... actions which don't come from faith, don't come from treasuring God over all things. And that's what sin *is*—not treasuring God above all things, preferring anything more than God.[19]

So it is true that your best work may, in fact, be a good deed, but only when looking at it from the perspective of it benefiting someone other than yourself. From a human angle, it *is* good. However, the predicament still remains that your work is tainted by your sin. At its very core, your deed is undeniably man-centered—which makes it 'a filthy garment' in the eyes of God. Every creature[20] in his or her present body is unable to perfectly perform the will of God. Remember what I said a few pages ago, that *we are unable to do a single sinless work in our own strength*. This is a truth that goes by the term 'original sin.'

Indeed, 'original sin' refers to *the* original sin—the first sin of Adam and Eve in the Garden of Eden. But it also involves the consequences of the act, which have been passed down through the entire human race. That is to say, mankind's make-up is marred. The whole person has now been affected by this defect. If you have a human mother and father (which you do!),[21] congrats, you are included

---

19. Piper, 'What is Sin? The Essence and Root of All Sinning.'

20. Genesis 1:27, 'God created man in His own image, in the image of God He created him; male and female He created them.'

21. Don't forget this as a crucial aspect of the sinless nature of Christ. He had no human father's seed to impregnate His human mother, the Virgin

in this transition—from a sinless state to a sinful one. The disease of depravity has been delivered from one person to another throughout all of human history. Everyone in your family tree fell right along with Adam and Eve. King David makes this crystal clear when writing in the book of Psalms, 'Behold, I was brought forth in iniquity, and in sin my mother conceived me' (51:5).[22]

The psalmist's words are painfully and personally true words. They describe the fallen nature that touches every part of us. Adam, Eve, the serpent, and all humanity received this curse as a result of their sin which began in Genesis 3.

Your good works (even your very best ones) cannot and are not inherently good, no matter how hard you try. Tough to hear, I know. But the whole truth remains that nobody is perfect, not even close. D.A. Carson quips that 'We live in an age where the one wrong thing to say is that somebody else is wrong.'[23]

Listen to how God responds to our sin: 'For the wrath of God is revealed from heaven against all ungodliness and unrighteousness of men who suppress the truth in

---

Mary. Yes, Jesus was born of a woman (a birth not unlike ours)—which demonstrates His humanity, but a baby was conceived in her womb by the supernatural power of the Holy Spirit (a miraculous conception, which was far different than ours).

22. David was not saying it was wrong for his father and mother to have conceived a child, nor was he making his birth out to be a sinful act in some way. Instead, this is a reference to his and our fallen nature. R.C Sproul said it best, 'The idea is: we are not sinners because we sin. But that we sin because we are sinners. We are, by nature, sinners.' (*Renewing Your Mind* radio broadcast from February 17, 2015, 'Total Depravity, Part One,' archived online at: http://renewingyourmind.org/2015/02/17/total-depravity-part-1.)

23. D. A. Carson, *Scandalous: The Cross and Resurrection of Jesus* (Wheaton: Crossway, 2010), 42.

unrighteousness,' (Rom. 1:18). What is our unrighteousness? Our lawlessness? Our sin? Paul lists them for us in the same letter of Romans (quoting from the Old Testament) in 3:10-18. If you have a Bible, feel free to open it and follow along:

- We are unrighteous: 'There is none righteous, not even one; there is no one who understands, no one who seeks God; all have turned aside, together they have become useless; there is no one who does good, there is not even one' (vv. 10-12; taken from Ps. 14:1-3; 53:1-3; Eccles. 7:20).

- We are unreliable: 'Their throat is an open grave, with their tongues they keep deceiving, the poison of asps [vipers] is under their lips,' (v. 13; taken from Ps. 5:9; 140:3).

- We are unsettling: 'Whose mouth is full of cursing and bitterness,' (v. 14; taken from Ps. 10:7).

- We are unscrupulous: 'Their feet are swift to shed blood, destruction and misery are in their paths, and the path of peace they have not known' (vv. 15-17; taken from Isa. 59:7-8).

- We are unafraid: 'There is no fear of God before their eyes' (v. 18; taken from Ps. 36:1).

What we've read is ruthless, right? Do you agree that the ways and works of man are far from righteous and warrant no hope of heaven? Left to ourselves, we are a moral mess. Pathetic. This disposition, a fallen nature, is the fundamental problem of all human history; our sin has stained it all. Every bit of it. Not a single work of ours can escape this problem.

D. A. Carson makes it even more personal:

[F]or many of us it is still difficult to feel empathy with Paul's stance… they seem a bit over the top, almost grotesque negativism. After all, you do not go around saying, 'I'm at the center of the universe.'

On the other hand, if someone were suddenly to hold up a picture of your graduating class from high school or college and say, 'This is your graduating class,' which face do you look for first—just to make sure it is there?

Or if you have an argument—a real humdinger, a knock-down-drag-'em-out-one-in-ten-years-argument, a real first-class roustabout argument—and you go away just seething, thinking of all the things that you could have said, all the things you should have said, all the things you would have said if you had thought of them fast enough, and then you replay the whole argument in your mind—who wins?

I have lost a lot of arguments in my time, but I have never lost a mental rerun.

The problem is that if I think that I am at the center of the universe, then most likely you do, too. And frankly, you stupid twit, how dare you set yourself up over against me? And now, instead of God being at the center, each human being, each of God's own image bearers, thinks he or she is at the center. We find our self-identity *not* in being God's creature, but in any other person, institution, value system, ritual—anything so that God cannot be heard, cannot be allowed to make His ultimate claim as our Creator and Judge… this stance means that I am now also in conflict with all these other people who want to be at the center of the universe, and there is the beginning of war, hate, rape, and fences—all because I say, 'I will be god.'[24]

Who is at the center of our efforts? The unholy trinity of me, myself, and I. With that kind of God-less attitude we will have absolutely no chance of Him declaring our works as good. 'God is opposed to the proud, but gives grace to the humble' (James 4:6). Our sin has separated us from what is truly good, and it has spoiled our efforts to get in His good graces. We are all guilty before God. What we need is reconciliation. We now have a debt before a holy and righteous Judge; and it is an infinite debt. Our sin will require all eternity in hell as payment for it, and the punishment will never be enough to satisfy the debt. Why is this the case? 'For whoever keeps the whole law and yet stumbles in one point, he has become guilty of all' (James 2:10). One single stumbling point = a failing grade for life.

CHRIST'S WORK

Do you see there is only one way to receive a passing grade in this life for the next? It cannot be done by placing your faith in a curve, in the works of sinful self. The celebrated twentieth-century preacher, Dr. Martyn-Lloyd Jones, delivered this same news to his congregation in 1941:

> Man must be convinced and convicted of his sin. He must face the naked, terrible truth about himself and his attitude towards God. It is only when he realizes that truth

---

24. Ibid, 44-45.

that he will be ready to believe the gospel and return to God.[25]

The pastor of Westminster Chapel pulled no punches in his London pulpit. He was on the offensive, observing how 'Philosophy has been glorified and man has claimed that he could solve the riddle of life and of the universe. Never has man been so proud of himself and his achievements and his understanding.'[26]

The grade is still the same. Man refuses to acknowledge his guilt before God, and so, paper after paper, year after year, it is returned with the wrong answer: 'I am saved by my good works.'

Hebrews 9:22 prescribes the process necessary in order for us to pass: 'without the shedding of blood there is no forgiveness.' We can be 'bought back' from the presence and power of our sin with a sacrifice. But for this to happen, we will need help. We need an offering to be made for our sins that meets the satisfaction of God. We are in need of a final and ultimate sacrifice. A penal substitution. Someone (a substitute) who is capable of taking the punishment (penal) for our offenses. It is a BIG ask! Our infinite offense requires a payment by an infinitely holy God.

Here is the good news[27]: the cross of Calvary is where our penalty for sin has been paid in full. Peter, in his first letter to his fellow Christians from Asia Minor, acknowledged this glorious truth—that Christ was the One who had

---

25. Dr. Martyn Lloyd-Jones, *The Plight of Man and the Power of God* (Ross-shire: Christian Focus Publications, 2010), 29.

26. Ibid, 105.

27. The good news is the gospel—literally! The Greek word for both nouns is εὐαγγέλιον.

completed this work: 'He Himself bore our sins in His body on the cross, so that we might die to sin and live to righteousness; for by His wounds you were healed' (1 Pet. 2:24). Paul recognized this too, when writing to the church in Rome: 'But God demonstrates His own love toward us, in that while we were yet sinners, Christ died for us' (Rom. 5:8).

Consider for a moment the stark contrast between what we had read earlier—condemning words from Paul (in Rom. 3:10-12), and Peter's here—on the work of the sinless One (from 1 Pet. 2:21-23):

- Christ's payment for us: 'since Christ also suffered for you' (v. 21b).

- Christ's purpose was us: 'leaving you an example for you to follow in His steps' (v. 21c).

- Christ's perfection, unlike us: 'Who committed no sin, nor was any deceit found in His mouth' (v. 22; taken from Isa. 53:9).

- Christ's patience with us: 'and while being reviled, He did not revile in return' (v. 23a).

- Christ's pledge because of us: 'while suffering, He uttered no threats, but kept entrusting Himself to Him who judges righteously' (v. 23b).

We have no good deeds of our own, no sinless works righteous enough to atone for our sins. It has been said that 'we are debtors who cannot pay their debts.'[28] An atonement had to be made on behalf of man if he was to have his fellowship restored with God, a fellowship

---

28. R.C. Sproul, *Essential Truths of the Christian Faith* (Carol Stream: Tyndale House Publishers, 1992), 181.

originally broken in the Garden.[29] Only the sinless Son of God could bear the wrath of God the Father upon the cross. He lived a perfect life and died a punishing death; it was a saving work for sinful man.

Galatians 3:13 reads, 'Christ redeemed us from the curse of the Law, having become a curse for us.' By doing so, He made His meritorious work available to 'all who will believe' (John 17:20). Freely available is this good and gracious work which must be received by faith. It cannot be earned by our own efforts. This is the only acceptable payment by God and from God for our penalty. When it was transacted Christ loudly proclaimed, 'It is finished!' (John 19:30).

But how can I be certain that the wrath of God upon my very soul has been satisfied? Where do I go to separate truth from error? (You know the answer.) This assurance can only be found in the trustworthy Word of God. Should you turn instead to man's religious manuals, you will be 'tossed here and there by waves and carried about by every wind of doctrine, by the trickery of men, by craftiness in deceitful scheming' (Eph. 4:14). It will ultimately prove to be a deadly affair. Don't get sucked in by the wisdom of this world with its half-truths. Put into practice some discernment so that you will be able to tell the difference between what is biblical and what is unbiblical. Go to God's Word for your answers.

The Bible states that the work of Christ on the cross *propitiated* His Father's judgment. 'Propitiation' essentially means a satisfactory act. It is defined as 'an offering that

---

29. Genesis 3:23-24, 'the Lord God sent him out from the Garden of Eden … so He drove man out.'

138

turns away the wrath of God directed against sin.'[30] Paul explains as much in Romans 3:23-25 when he says, 'for all have sinned and fall short of the glory of God, being justified [literally, 'pardoned from punishment' or 'declared righteous'] as a gift by His grace through the redemption which is in Christ Jesus; whom God displayed publicly as a propitiation in His blood through faith.' It is the death of the sinless Son of God that satisfied the Father's requirement for our sin. The Bible tells us that nothing else comes even close.

Hebrews 2:17 corroborates this. There we read, 'Therefore, He had to be made like His brethren in all things [human], so that He might become a merciful and faithful high priest in things pertaining to God, to make propitiation for the sins of the people.' Christ was our substitute in every possible way. He was human in every way we are, except sinlessly so—a perfect substitution. It was this perfect life, sacrificed for sinners by a punishing death, which appeased the Father's wrath.

Furthermore, 'the resurrection was God's seal of approval on the propitiation Christ offered.' John MacArthur writes that it 'is the seal and the linchpin of gospel truth.'[31] Without the resurrection, our faith in the sin-satisfying work of Christ would be in vain. If Christ had remained dead, His work would have meant nothing more than yours or mine. It would be just another death, just another work. We would

---

30. Grenz, Guretzki, and Nordling, *Pocket Dictionary of Theological Terms,* 96.

31. John MacArthur's *Grace to You* blog post: *Paul's Gospel Essentials: Resurrection and Eyewitnesses*, March 2, 2017. Accessed at: https://www.gty.org/library/blog/B170302/.

have no cause to trust in it. The grade would still have been a failing one. Literally, it would have been pointless.

Paul addresses this directly with the Corinthians when he writes, 'If Christ has not been raised, your faith is worthless; you are still in your sins' (1 Cor. 15:17). The resurrection is proof-positive of this propitiation. God had a different plan. He would secure those who are 'pierced to the heart' (Acts 2:37) with a glorious gospel truth: God the Father raised God the Son from the grave, through the power of the Holy Spirit, to declare to a watching world that Jesus was the one who could pay for sin. Jesus is the *only* one worthy of our faith. By being raised from the dead, the sinless Savior offers forgiveness to any-and-all who will *repent* of their sin and *believe* in His work at Calvary.

> *Are you convicted of your need to do so*
> *while reading this chapter?*
> *Will you confess that you are a sinner of*
> *no-good works in need of saving?*
> *Do you believe His work upon the cross*
> *paid for your sins: past, present, and future?*

He is the only valid Object of your saving faith. He is the only viable Substitute for your sin.

Paul writes, 'If you will confess with your mouth Jesus as Lord, and believe in your heart that God raised Him from the dead, you will be saved' (Rom. 10:9). Don't miss this: the gospel has the power to save sinners. I am one of them who has been redeemed by this wondrous work from the Son of God. The forgiveness of your sin, along with a reconciliation and peace with God, can all be yours by faith alone.

Sincerely, as I write this I am praying you are willing and able to confess, repent, believe, and rejoice with me as a brother or sister in the family of 'God through our Lord Jesus Christ, through whom we have now received the reconciliation … For as through the one man's disobedience the many were made sinners, even so through the obedience of the One the many will be made righteous' (Rom. 5:11, 19). If you have not already done so, I plead with you to cry out to God for mercy and receive His gift of saving grace today.

THE WHOLE MEANING

What have we covered so far in this chapter? It can be answered by a single verse dealing with salvation: 'With people this is impossible, but with God all things are possible' (Matt. 19:26). We have explored the fallacies of trusting in man's 'good' works to enter and experience the joys of heaven (impossible), and the true faith that is necessary to receive Christ's work (possible). Coming full circle, we must ask the question, 'Do our good works matter at all before God?'

The answer for the believer in Christ is a resounding 'yes!' Our faith in Him will produce good works. God declares them good works because they glorify Him and not ourselves. From His 'Sermon on the Mount,' Jesus says 'Let your light shine before men in such a way that they may see your good works, and glorify your Father who is in heaven' (5:16). This is why James wrote, 'Even so faith, if it has no works, is dead, being by itself.' No works mean no faith. In other words, 'a deedless faith is not saving faith. To miss this point is to ignore the forest while staring at a

141

single tree.'[32] Those good works are only possible because of faith.

Think of it this way. If you are a believer in Christ, then you should be able to look back at your life as a Christian and see growth. Your faith will produce godly growth over a period of time. Perhaps a few weeks, some months, even years—but the idea is that your faith is developing godliness from the inside out. Your faith will bear fruit from the Spirit of God which resides in you. What kind of fruit?

> But the fruit of the Spirit is love, joy, peace, patience, kindness, goodness, faithfulness, gentleness, self-control … [you will] pursue righteousness, godliness, faith, love, perseverance and gentleness … [you will be] hospitable, loving what is good, sensible, just, devout, self-controlled, holding fast the faithful Word which is in accordance with the teaching … able both to exhort in sound doctrine and to refute those who contradict. (Gal. 5:22-23; 1 Tim. 6:11; Titus 1:8-9)

Your new life in Christ should yield good works which will 'proclaim the excellencies of Him who has called you out of darkness into His marvelous light' (1 Pet. 2:9). Without this faith, a work is just that, a work. But with it, a work is a result of that faith which will in turn glorify God. 'My Father is glorified by this, that you bear much fruit, and so prove to be My disciples' (John 15:8).

---

32. While it is not my intent to unpack James 2:14-26, James R. White masterfully does so in his book *The God Who Justifies: The Doctrine of Justification* (Minneapolis: Bethany House Publishers, 2001), 331-332. White begins the chapter by saying the passage 'can be summarized by the words "show me" … This exhortation of Christians is not addressing how the ungodly are declared righteous before God [because they are not], but how that declaration is shown outwardly in the Christian life' 329.

Alistair Begg uses a helpful analogy in his book, *What Angels Wished They Knew*:[33]

> Consider a bottle of penicillin, the famous antibiotic identified by Alexander Fleming, and first produced for clinical use at the Radcliffe Infirmary, Oxford, and responsible for saving the lives of countless individuals who would otherwise have died from various forms of blood poisoning. Imagine that—
>
> a. this bottle is sitting on my bedside table, and that—
> b. I am suffering from blood poisoning
>
> What are my options?
>
> a. I may *accept* that this bottle of penicillin exists.
> b. I may *trust* that it is capable of curing my illness, which otherwise will probably kill me. But I shall never cure my blood poisoning, unless—
> c. I *act* upon that trust and take the penicillin. Acceptance and trust prepare the way for the final component of faith—entering into the promise and receiving what it offers. I may accept that the bottle exists, and I may trust in its ability to cure blood poisoning—but unless I take the drug which it contains, I have not benefited from my faith in it. I shall die, accepting and trusting,

---

33. From Alister McGrath, *Bridge-Building*, as quoted in Alistair Begg's *What Angels Wished They Knew: The Basics of True Christianity* (Chicago: Moody Press, 1998), 168-169.

> but having failed to benefit at all from the
> resource which could have saved me.

Your faith must be a genuine faith. Having a head knowledge may mean that you have been deemed as smart, but not necessarily wise. Beware: a lot of smart people will go to hell. Your 'good' works cannot come first; they must be preceded by a genuine faith. Stop. Drop. And examine your heart to see it is a real faith. This is no drill. Check yourself, for it must be a wholehearted faith that is useful, fruitful, and thankful to the One who saved you.

SUMMARY

- **The Half-Truth:** Our good deeds matter. Like professors who inflate their students' grades, there is a belief that people will get to heaven as a result of God grading on a scale. But our good deeds will never merit salvation. Man has devised a vast number of religious and secular ways to save himself. Sadly, they will all lead to his eternal destruction.

- **The Whole-Truth:** Our good deeds matter, *when preceded by faith*. There are only two types of works: human achievement and divine accomplishment. Your answer on God's final exam will be predicated upon what you believe merits a passing grade. It will either be man-centered or Christ-centered. Man's works have been stained by Original Sin, while Christ's work on the cross propitiated the wrath of God. There is no curve, only the cross. Which work will you place your faith in?

- **The Whole Meaning:** Your new life in Christ should yield good works that glorify God, not the other way around. Works will never produce salvation or promote self. Check your heart! This is as serious as it gets. Remember, 'good' works cannot come first. They must be preceded by a genuine faith—one that will bear fruit from (the Spirit of) God which resides in you.

6.
THE WHOLE TRUTH

MY JOURNEY

Those five half-truths were my truths. Frequently, I would use them to deflect and deceive myself, as well as others who had wanted to discuss them. Can you see what is missing from each of them now?

The Bible was written by men … *and inspired by God.*
All religions are the same … *except Christianity.*
God is love … *and holy, holy, holy.*
Jesus is truly a man … *and truly God.*
And our good deeds matter … *when preceded by faith.*

I can still remember the moment I learned that these five half-truths had kept me from the whole truth. For at that very moment I was born again. When I was rescued from the empty deception of human wisdom and supernaturally introduced to God's wisdom, literally, I was 'born from above.'

This is what is known as the new birth—the life of God entering into the soul of a man. Spiritually, I had been dead in my trespasses and sins, but God gave me new eyes to see, new ears to hear, and a new heart to believe His glorious truth. He had changed me to a newness of life in Jesus Christ. It was amazing grace, indeed.

This all started back in 1993 while working in a New York radio station. A disc jockey named Barbara had quickly earned the reputation as our resident 'Jesus freak.' I was warned by co-workers not to engage her in truth-seeking debates, which only encouraged me to do so. As I share this—I am so grateful that she politely and firmly challenged me in our conversations. Barbara never backed away from the terse words I had become so accustomed to delivering as insults. They were defense mechanisms that I would throw out as half-truths about the Bible, presenting them as whole truths. But she would not let me get away with that. Not one bit. Nope. Instead, she challenged me to look up the real answers for myself.

For example, I love history and was astounded to learn that the Bible was not translated by 'a bunch of old men' (as I had asserted), but rather it has more manuscript evidence than any of the classical works I was required to read in school! Homer's *Iliad* and Plato's *Tetralogies* are not even in the same ballpark when compared with the number of New Testament manuscripts.

Another truth I had learned, from an evidential perspective, deals with the apostle Peter and the death sentence he received for sharing the gospel. Tradition tells us that Peter, before being crucified, was forced to watch the crucifixion of his wife. Fourth-century church historian Eusebius wrote:

'he stood at the foot of his wife's cross and kept repeating to her, "Remember the Lord, remember the Lord." And after she had died, he himself was crucified and pleaded to be crucified upside down because he was unworthy to die like his Lord.'[1]

I had come to realize that the Bible *is* the very Word of God. Christianity's claims are exclusive, not inclusive. God is love, yes—but He is also holy, holy, holy and must judge sin. That is why He sent His one and only Son to redeem us from its power and penalty. Our works are unable to save us, but our faith in the One who already did the work on the cross does. He paid it all. This is the whole truth.

And so it was in that radio station during a commercial break that I prayed out loud to God. Barbara had recognized that I was broken over my sin and desired a right relationship with Him. She had helped me to see my most pressing need: that I can trust God and His Word. Now I needed to place my faith in Christ alone for the forgiveness of my sin and newness of life. For Jesus is who He said He was: 'I am the Light of the world; he who follows Me will not walk in the darkness, but will have the Light of life' (John 8:12).

Today, I invite you to join me in doing the same. You have been presented with the whole truth, too. In fact, these previous five chapters have each revealed a *half-truth*, unveiled a specific *whole truth*, and then explained its *whole meaning*. Only one question remains: will you repent of your sin and believe in Jesus Christ as your Savior? (It certainly would make for a happy ending.)

---

1. Eusebius, *Ecclesiastical History*, 3:1, 30. Accessed online at: http://www.newadvent.org/fathers/250103.htm.

I am reminded of James' words in 4:7-10:

Submit therefore to God. Resist the devil and he will flee from you. Draw near to God and He will draw near to you. Cleanse your hands, you sinners; and purify your hearts, you double-minded. Be miserable and mourn and weep; let your laughter be turned into mourning and your joy to gloom. Humble yourselves in the presence of the Lord, and He will exalt you.

7.

THINKING IT THROUGH

YOUR CHALLENGE

Everything I have said in this book was intended to fulfill two objectives: to present Christ rightly through Scripture, and to plead for your repentance earnestly in this brief window of time we have together. If you believe Jesus to be the promised Messiah, the Son of God, your Savior—then you must first receive Him. We read, 'But as many as received Him, to them He gave the right to become children of God, even to those who believe in His Name' (John 1:12).

Have you done so? This opportunity might never be yours again, for we do not know what tomorrow holds. (If you are not ready to receive Christ, please keep reading.) But if you have received Christ, let me help you below with a simple guide as to some suggested next steps in your spiritual journey.

Did you know that by reading through the five previous chapters—five half-truths—that you have also completed a brief academic study in systematic theology? It may not have seemed like it, but you did. Systematic theology uniquely arranges biblical doctrines (teachings) by categories:

- *Bibliology* is the study of the nature and character of the Bible as it relates to inspiration, inerrancy, authority, sufficiency, etc. The first half-truth was *Concerning the Bible* (ch. 1). It covered exactly this from the perspective of playing the telephone game.

- *Christology* is the study of the Person and work of Jesus Christ. The second half-truth, *Concerning Christianity* (ch. 2), and the third, *Concerning Christ* (ch. 4), both addressed key elements of His human and divine natures, as well as His miraculous works.

- *Theology Proper* is the study of God Himself. The third half-truth, *Concerning God* (ch. 3), looked specifically at His attributes of love, grace, and holiness.

- *Soteriology* is the study of salvation, *hamartiology* is the study of sin, and *anthropology* is the study of man. Each of these doctrines were explored in the fifth half-truth, *Concerning Faith* (ch. 5).

Any study of Christian theology is time well-spent, as theologian David Wells writes, 'in order that we might know Him, learn to think our thoughts after Him, live our lives in His world on His terms, and by thought and action project His truth into our own time and culture.'[1] Your

---

1. From David Wells, 'The Theologian's Craft,' in *Doing Theology in Today's World: Essays in Honor of Kenneth S. Kantzer*, as quoted in *Biblical Doctrine:*

challenge moving forward is to not stop exploring these truths of God's Word. Below are three ways to continue to accomplish this—to help further your spiritual growth.

PURCHASE A STUDY BIBLE

First, I would recommend purchasing a sound study Bible. This is a Bible that has explanatory notes printed along with the text of Scripture. You will also find them to have incredibly helpful charts, maps, and photos throughout its pages. *The MacArthur Study Bible* is where I would begin, and you can choose from a handful of core translations (such as the New American Standard Bible, known as the NASB, the English Standard Version [ESV], the New International Version [NIV], and the New King James Version [NKJV]). Visit *Grace to You* online at gty.org to learn more. There are also a number of other helpful study Bibles out there, such as *The Reformation Study Bible*, *The ESV Study Bible*, and *The NIV Zondervan Study Bible*.

READ GOD'S WORD

Second, I'd like to challenge you to resolve to read your Bible daily. Does your morning (or evening) routine need to change? This is an intentional way to learn from and love God more. And don't take for granted the opportunity to be doing this with others. Accountability and encouragement help us to go the distance when we are tempted to quit, get sick, or become overwhelmed by life. Invite your family and friends to join you on this journey.

A Systematic Summary of Bible Truth, ed. John MacArthur and Richard Mayhue (Wheaton: Crossway, 2017), 34.

If you have never read a portion of Scripture before, let me suggest you begin with the Gospel of John. *The MacArthur Study Bible* has a one-year reading plan listed in the back. There are also a variety of plans available online. What is important is that you *begin*. Pick a place in the home to regularly read God's Word. Get the coffee ready, lay out your Bible and materials the night before. Don't check the sports scores, or social media when you awake—read first. Otherwise, they rob you of your precious and always-evaporating morning time.

What's most important for the true worshiper of God is to be reading His Word *daily*. The psalmist says of the godly person, 'his delight is in the law of the Lord, and in His law he meditates day and night' (Ps. 1:2). Jonathan Edwards also recognized the value of making time for the reading of Scripture (by the way, we never 'find' time, we must 'make' it). In 1722, he penned his 28th resolution which reads, 'Resolved: to study the Scriptures so steadily, constantly, and frequently, that I may find, and plainly perceive myself to grow in the knowledge of them.'[2]

READ GOOD BOOKS

Third, read good books. Tony Reinke is right when he writes, 'There are always interruptions and other things to do. We can all find excuses for why we cannot read... But we all find time to do what we 'want' to do.'[3] Sadly, we are grooming an entire subset of Christians who rarely read.

---

2. *Jonathan Edwards' Resolutions and Advice to Young Converts*, ed. Stephen J. Nichols (Phillipsburg: P&R Publishing, 2001), 20.

3. Tony Reinke, *Lit! A Christian Guide to Reading Books* (Wheaton: Crossway, 2011), 132.

Yes, it is hard work, but for whatever reason (and there are many), people are not making the investment where it really counts—on the inside. They have grown weak by not flexing their reading muscles. Reinke adds, 'The problem is not that we don't have *time* to read, but that we don't have the *desire* to read. So learn to love reading—because it's easier to find time to do what you love to do.'

Nowhere do we see this played out more than on our mobile devices. In this digital age we are more apt to scroll down a social media feed than to unplug and read critically.[4] 'Find books that grab you. Read the books that make you lose sleep at night. Perhaps that's a book that you have already read. Reread it.'[5] Yes, a good book is read more than once!

Here are five books at the top of my list:

1. *The Holiness of God*, by R.C. Sproul (Tyndale House Publishers, 1985)

   Book description: Central to God's character is the quality of holiness. Yet, even so, most people are hard-pressed to define what God's holiness precisely is. Many preachers today avoid the topic altogether because people today don't quite know what to do with words like 'awe' or 'fear.' R. C. Sproul, in this classic work, puts the holiness of God in its proper and central place in the Christian life. He paints an awe-inspiring vision of God that encourages Christians to become holy just as

---

4. If you are interested in learning more on the impact technology is having upon us—good and bad—let me recommend Tony Reinke's book *12 Ways Your Phone is Changing You* (Wheaton: Crossway, 2017).

5. Reinke, *Lit! A Christian Guide to Reading Books*, 132.

God is holy. Once you encounter the holiness of God, your life will never be the same.

2. *Hard to Believe: The High Cost and Infinite Value of Following Jesus,* by John MacArthur (Thomas Nelson, 2003)

   Book description: Jesus Christ did not die on the cross so you and I could have a nice day. Ministers and teachers who water down the gospel of Christ in order to make it more popular and appealing may be leading their fun-loving audiences down the road to eternal punishment.

   This book is John MacArthur's unflinching, unapologetic treatise on the modern tendency to alter the true message of Christianity in order to meet the whims and desires of a culture hoping for nonconfrontational messages, easy answers, and superficial commitments. Too many people just want a Madison Avenue Jesus to make them well, make them happy, and make them prosperous. But Jesus Christ isn't a personal genie. He is the Savior; He died in agony to satisfy the wrath of a holy God and to forgive the sins of humankind. Faith in Him demands a willingness to make any sacrifice He asks. The hard truth about Christianity is that the cost is high, but the rewards are priceless—abundant and eternal life that comes only from faithfully following Christ.

3. *Finally Alive,* by John Piper (Christian Focus Publications, 2001)

Book description: When Jesus said to Nicodemus, 'You must be born again', the devout and learned religious leader was unsure what Jesus meant. It would seem nothing has changed. Today 'born again Christians' fill churches that are seen as ineffectual at best, and even characterized by the 'mosaic' generation as 'unchristian.' The term 'born again' has been devalued both in society and in the church. Those claiming to be 'born again' live lives that are indistinguishable from those who don't; they sin the same, embrace injustice the same, covet the same, do almost everything the same. Being 'born again' is now defined by what people say they believe. The New Testament however defines Christians very differently.

4. *In It To Win It: Pursuing Victory in the One Race That Really Counts,* by Steven J. Lawson (Harvest House Publishers, 1992)

    Book description: What believer doesn't want to succeed in the Christian life? God's desire is for His people to experience real success—the kind that lasts into eternity and not the world's fleshly substitute. With the help of athletic illustrations both from Scripture and real life, you will learn what it takes to be your best by discovering …

    - what it really means to put God first in all things
    - how to live the Christian life in God's power
    - the essentials for building spiritual endurance
    - effective ways to avoid hindrances and temptation

- the keys to making the best choices and finishing strong

Winning with God makes you a winner in every area of life. No matter what your occupation or background, the principles in this book will enable you to experience God's kind of success—a success that will have a positive impact on all you do.

5. *The Man Christ Jesu Theological Reflections on the Humanity of Christ*, by Bruce Ware (Crossway, 2013)

Book description: What does it mean for Jesus to be HUMAN? Theologian Bruce Ware takes us back to the biblical text, where we meet a profoundly human Jesus who faced many of the same difficulties and limitations we experience today. Ware explores the significance of Christ's humanity and helps us to learn, by the power of the Spirit, to follow in Jesus' steps.

Please take a moment to let me know what you thought of this book, as well as your next steps so that I can be faithfully praying for you. The challenge is the same for each of us: may we be found faithful to 'grow in the grace and knowledge of our Lord and Savior Jesus Christ. To Him be the glory, both now and to the day of eternity' (2 Pet. 3:18).

Christian Focus Publications

Our mission statement –

STAYING FAITHFUL

In dependence upon God we seek to impact the world through literature faithful to His infallible Word, the Bible. Our aim is to ensure that the Lord Jesus Christ is presented as the only hope to obtain forgiveness of sin, live a useful life and look forward to heaven with Him.

Our books are published in four imprints:

CHRISTIAN FOCUS

Popular works including biographies, commentaries, basic doctrine and Christian living.

CHRISTIAN HERITAGE

Books representing some of the best material from the rich heritage of the church.

MENTOR

Books written at a level suitable for Bible College and seminary students, pastors, and other serious readers. The imprint includes commentaries, doctrinal studies, examination of current issues and church history.

CF4·K

Children's books for quality Bible teaching and for all age groups: Sunday school curriculum, puzzle and activity books; personal and family devotional titles, biographies and inspirational stories – because you are never too young to know Jesus!

Christian Focus Publications Ltd,
Geanies House, Fearn, Ross-shire,
IV20 1TW, Scotland, United Kingdom.
www.christianfocus.com
blog.christianfocus.com